Window

Visual Quick Reference

Michael Watson

Windows 95 Visual Quick Reference

Library of Congress Catalog No.: 95-70644

ISBN: 1-56529-930-2

97 96 95   6 5 4 3 2 1

Interpretation of the printing code: the rightmost double-digit number is the year of the book's printing; the rightmost single-digit number, the number of the book's printing. For example, a printing code of 95-1 shows that the first printing of the book occurred in 1995.

Screen reproductions in this book were created using Collage Plus from Inner Media, Inc., Hollis, NH.

Credits

President
Roland Elgey

Vice President and Publisher
Marie Butler-Knight

Associate Publishers
Don Roche, Jr.
Joseph B. Wikert

Editorial Services Director
Elizabeth Keaffaber

Managing Editor
Michael Cunningham

Director of Marketing
Lynn E. Zingraf

Senior Series Editor
Chris Nelson

Acquisitions Editor
Deborah F. Abshier

Product Directors
Joyce J. Neilsen
Robin Drake

Production Editor
Lori A. Lyons

Assistant Product Marketing Manager
Kim Margolius

Technical Editors
Robert Bogue
Jeffrey Scott
Robin Schreier

Technical Specialist
Cari Skaggs

Acquisitions Coordinator
Tracy M. Williams

Operations Coordinator
Patty Brooks

Editorial Assistants
Carmen Phelps
Jill Byus

Book Designers
Kim Scott
Sandra Schroeder

Cover Designer
Jay Corpus

Production Team
Claudia Bell, Amy Cornwell,
Anne Dickerson, DiMonique
Ford, John Hulse, Beth
Lewis, Damon Jordan, Clair
Schweinler, Michael Thomas,
Kelly Warner

Indexer
Mary Jane Frisby

Composed in *Stone Serif* and *Helvetica* by Que Corporation

About the Author

Formerly an engineer and designer of computer-controlled machine tools, **Michael Watson** is principal of Archetype Communications, a firm offering professional services to the computer publishing trade. He is revision author of *Easy DOS 6.2* and coauthor of *Windows VisiRef, 3.11 Edition*. Michael has also performed technical editing on more than 75 titles from Que.

Dedication

To Connie, my love and best friend.

Acknowledgments

To everyone who sweat over this one. Thank you.

Trademarks

All terms mentioned in this book that are known to be trademarks or service marks have been appropriately capitalized. Que cannot attest to the accuracy of this information. Use of a term in this book should not be regarded as affecting the validity of any trademark or service mark.

Contents

1 How To Use This Book   **1**

2 Accessories: Calculator, Notepad, Paint, WordPad   **3**

Using Windows Productivity Accessories 3
    To start and close an accessory program 3
Using Calculator 3
Using Notepad 5
    To use Notepad 5
    To copy and paste text 6
    To find text 7
    To print a file 8
    To save a file 8
Using Paint 10
    To use Paint 10
    To fill a shape with color .12
    To use the brush 12
    To draw a line 13
    To erase part of a drawing 13
    To insert text 14
    To erase a selected area .14
    To print a file 15
    To save a file 16
Using WordPad 17
    To use WordPad 17
    To copy and paste text 18
    To select text 19
    To boldface selected text .19
    To italicize selected text .19
    To underline selected text 20
    To change the color of selected text 20
    To left-align selected text 20
    To center selected text 21
    To right-align selected text 21
    To change the font of selected text 21
    To change the font size of selected text 22

To insert a bullet 23
To find text 23
To print a file 24
To save a file 24

3 Basics: Starting/Exiting, Screen Elements, Mouse   27

Starting and Exiting Windows 27
To start Windows 27
To exit Windows 28
Parts of the Windows screen 29
Mouse Operations 29
To point and click 29
To double-click 30
To move a window by dragging 30
To resize a window by dragging 31
Arranging Icons 32
Opening a Window or Application 32
To open an application or window
from a menu 32
To open an application or window
from a window 33
Closing a Window 33
Selecting a Window 33
Minimizing and Maximizing Windows 34
To minimize a window 34
To maximize a window 34
To restore a maximized window 34

4 Communications: HyperTerminal, Phone Dialer, Mail   35

Using Windows Communications Accessories 35
To start and close an accessory program 35
Using HyperTerminal 35
To start HyperTerminal 36
To create a new connection 36
To use a connection 41
To upload a file 42
To download a file 43

To capture text from the HyperTerminal
window 44
To stop text capture 45
To disconnect from the remote system 45
Using Phone Dialer 46
To use Phone Dialer 46
Using the Microsoft Mail Postoffice 47

5 Customizing: Screen, Fonts, Passwords, Dates   49

Using the Windows Control Panel 49
Installing and Uninstalling Application Programs 49
Adding and Removing Windows Components 51
Changing the Look of the Windows Desktop 53
To add a background pattern 53
To set up wallpaper 54
To turn the screen saver on or off 54
To change colors and fonts 55
To change the display settings 56
Adding Fonts 56
Setting Up Passwords for Security 57
To add passwords on a networked system 58
Setting the Date, Time, and Time Zone 60
To set the date or time 60
To set the time zone 61
Changing the Regional Settings 62
To change the number format 62
To change the currency format 63
To change the time format 63
To change the date format 64
Assigning Sounds to System Events 64

6 Disk Management: Disks, Folders, and Formatting   67

Managing Folders 67
To create a folder 67
To delete a folder 68
Working with Floppy Disks .69
To format a floppy disk 70
Copying a Floppy Disk 71

7 DOS Programs: Commands and Properties   73

Running DOS Commands 73
Running DOS Applications .74
Editing DOS Application Properties 76
   To configure general properties 76
   To configure program properties 77
   To change the program's default font settings 77
   To change the memory settings for the program . . .78
   To change the screen settings 78
   To configure miscellaneous application
   properties 79

8 Equipment: Installation and Setup   81

Adding New Hardware 81
Creating a Startup Disk 82
Configuring the Keyboard .83
   To set the delay and repeat 83
   To change the keyboard language 84
   To set the keyboard type .84
Configuring Modems 85
   To set modem properties .85
Configuring the Mouse 88
   To change the button settings 88
   To select a new pointer scheme 89
   To configure mouse motion 89
   To install a different mouse 90
Configuring Multimedia Properties 91
   To configure audio properties 91
   To change the video properties 92
   To set up MIDI output 92
   To change the CD-ROM drive volume settings 93
   To configure advanced properties 93
Configuring the Network 94
   To set component properties 94
   To change the identification settings 95
   To configure access control for security 95
Configuring Printers 96
   To set general printer properties 97
   To configure port and timeout settings 97
   To allow printer sharing .98

To set up paper size and orientation 98
To control print quality for graphics 99
To configure fonts 99
To configure additional device options 100
Changing System Properties 100
To configure devices 101
To create new hardware profiles 101
To improve system performance 102
Configuring Accessibility Options 105
To select keyboard options 105
To choose sound options 106
To set the display to high contrast 106
To control the mouse with the 10-key pad 107
To configure general options 107

9 Files and Folders: Working with Explorer   109

Using Windows Explorer 109
To start Windows Explorer 109
To expand the view of a drive 110
To expand the view of a folder 111
To open a file 112
To print a file 113
To preview a file 114
To send a file as a fax 115
To send a file as a mail message 115
To copy a file 116
To create a shortcut 117
To delete a file 117
To restore a deleted file .118
To rename a file or folder 119
To view or set file properties 120
To add a program shortcut to the Programs
menu 121
Finding Files 123
To search by name and location 123
To search by date modified 124
To search with advanced criteria 125
Associating Files with Programs 126
Changing the Explorer View 127
To display with large icons 127

To display with small icons 127
To display a listing 128
To display details 128
To sort the display 128

10 Help: Getting Information about Windows Tasks   129

Getting Help on the Desktop 129
To use the Help Index 129
To use the Table of Contents 130
Getting Help in a Dialog Box 132
To get help in a dialog box 132
To get information in a dialog box 133
Getting Help in a Window .134
Getting Help with an Object 135

11 Microsoft Exchange: Using the Inbox   137

Using the Inbox 137
To read a message 138
To save the message 139
To reply to a message 139
To forward the message .140
To delete a message 142
To send a new message .142
To send a fax 144
To set Inbox options 148

12 Microsoft Network: MSN Central, Bulletin Boards   151

Using the Microsoft Network 151
To connect to Microsoft Network 151
To access MSN Today 153
To use e-mail 154
To use items stored in Favorite Places 155
To use Member Assistance services 156
To read the bulletin boards 157
To read a bulletin board message 159
To post a bulletin board message 160

13 Multimedia: Audio CD, Sound, MIDI, Video   163

Using Windows Multimedia Accessories 163
  To start and close an accessory program 163
Using CD Player 163
  To create a play list .164
  To control CD Player .165
Using Media Player 165
  To play a media file .165
  To control Media Player 167
Using Sound Recorder .167
  To operate Sound Recorder 167
  To control Sound Recorder 168
  To add effects 168
  To save a sound file .169
Using Volume Control .169
  To operate Volume Control 169

14 Printing: Printing Files and Controlling Printers   171

Printing a File 171
  To print a file by dragging and dropping 171
Controlling Your Print Jobs 172
  To pause a print job .172
  To resume printing a paused print job 173
  To cancel a print job .174
  To check the status of print jobs 175
  To purge print jobs 175

15 System Maintenance: Backup, DriveSpace, ScanDisk   177

Using the Windows System Accessories 177
Using Backup 177
  To make a backup 177
  To restore from a backup 180
Defragmenting Disks with Disk Defragmenter 181
Using DriveSpace 183
Scanning a Disk for Errors with ScanDisk 185
  To perform a complete scan 185
  To customize the scan 187

Index   188

Introduction

How To Use This Book

Welcome to a new concept in quick references! Unlike traditional pocket references, which usually pack a lot of text on the page but few, if any, illustrations, the *Visual Quick Reference* series presents much of its "how-to" information in a visual manner.

This reference is task-oriented, and categories of tasks are organized alphabetically so that you can find them quickly. Use the different category sections to locate the task you want, follow the screen shots to see each step in the process, and then complete the task yourself.

If you prefer to learn or recall information by being shown how a task is accomplished, Que's *Windows 95 Visual Quick Reference* is well-matched to your needs. This book is the perfect complement to Windows and its graphical interface; you don't have to read a lot of text to find the reference information you need.

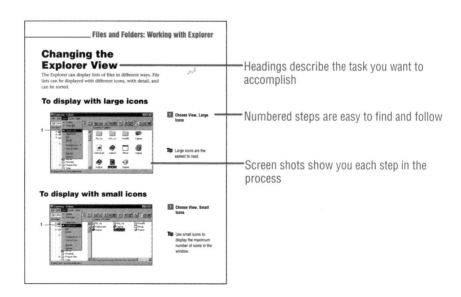

Headings describe the task you want to accomplish

Numbered steps are easy to find and follow

Screen shots show you each step in the process

Using Windows Productivity Accessories

These accessories are small applications that are bundled with Windows. Typically, accessories are run from the Start menu. Note that Windows also includes other accessories that are not covered in this section; the system accessories are covered in the section "System Maintenance" later in this book.

To start and close an accessory program

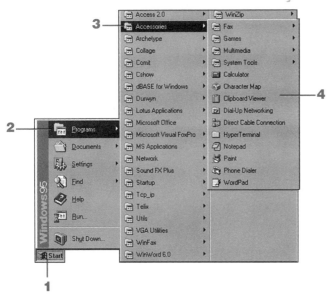

1 Click Start

2 Click Programs

3 Click Accessories

4 Click the name of the program you want

5 When you finish with the accessory program, click the Close button

Using Calculator

The Calculator performs mathematical operations, like a hand-held calculator. It incorporates both basic and scientific functions and uses Windows cut and paste features.

To switch to a scientific-style calculator, choose View, Scientific

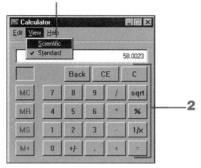

1 Choose Start,
Programs,
Accessories,
Calculator

2 Click keys to calculate
as desired

Note

Using the Calculator may take a little practice. You can click the numbers or use your computer's 10-key pad. The following table describes the mathematical symbols you use. To store numbers in memory, use the buttons that begin with M. For more details, choose Help.

Calculator symbol	Function
+	Addition
−	Subtraction
*	Multiplication
/	Division

Tip If you make a mistake while typing, click C or press Esc to clear the entry line.

Tip You can use the Edit, Copy and Edit, Paste commands to move numbers between Calculator and another application.

4

Using Notepad

Notepad will load nearly any small file for display or editing. It is typically used for editing ASCII text files and does not apply any formatting to the text.

To use Notepad

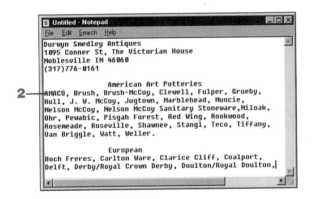

1 Choose Start, Programs, Accessories, Notepad

2 Enter and edit text as desired

Tip If you make a mistake while editing, immediately choose Edit, Undo to reverse the last action.

Caution You will see a warning message if you try to load a file that is too big for Notepad to hold.

5

To copy and paste text

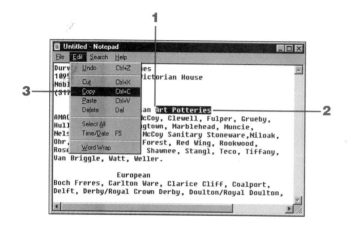

1 Click the starting point

2 Drag to the end of the desired text

3 Choose Edit, Copy or press Ctrl+C

Tip To delete marked text, choose Edit, Cut. The deleted text may be pasted elsewhere if desired.

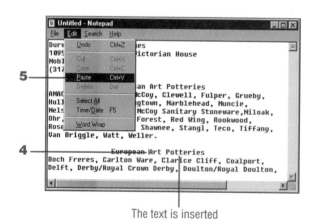

The text is inserted

4 Click the insertion point

5 Choose Edit, Paste or press Ctrl+V

To find text

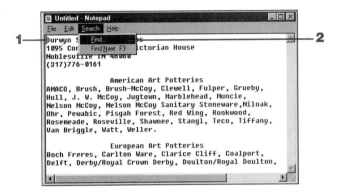

1 Click at the beginning of the document

2 Choose Search, Find

The found text is highlighted

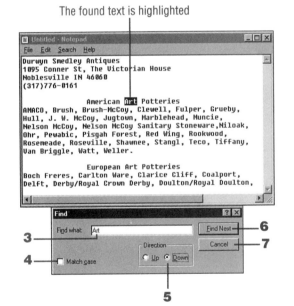

3 Enter the text to search for

4 Click to match case, if desired

5 Click to change direction, if necessary

6 Click Find Next— repeat until you find the text you want

7 Click Cancel

Tip Notepad displays an error message if the requested text is not found.

To print a file

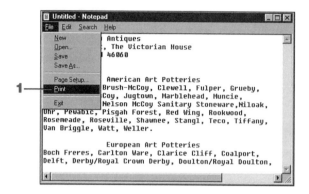

The file is sent to the printer

1 Choose File, Print

Note

Because there are no printing options to select, choosing File, Print immediately sends the file to the printer. A dialog box offers you a Cancel command button, but most memo-length files are sent to the printer so quickly that they cannot be canceled.

To save a file

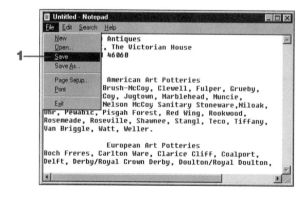

1 Choose File, Save

Tip If you have not saved the file before, follow the steps on the next page.

Tip To open an existing text file with Notepad, choose File, Open and select the file you want to open.

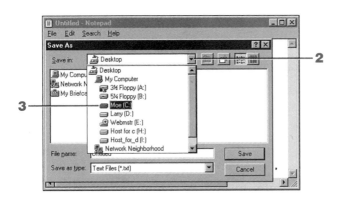

2 Click the drop-down button

3 Click a drive icon or Network Neighborhood

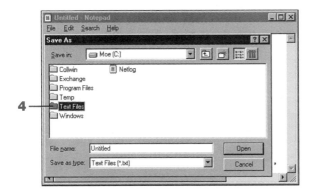

4 Double-click a destination folder (repeat until you have the right folder)

5 Type a file name

6 Click Save

Tip Windows 95 allows you to use long file names. You are not limited to eight-character file names and three-character extensions. You may include spaces in file names.

Using Paint

Bitmapped image files may be created, edited, and saved with Paint. Many drawing "tools" are available to create simple or complex shapes in different colors. Paint files may be printed on graphics-capable printers.

To use Paint

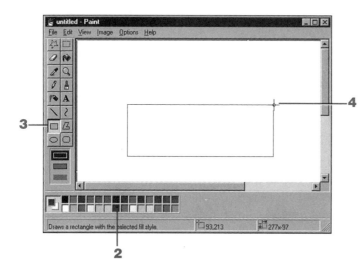

1 Choose Start, Programs, Accessories, Paint

2 Click a color

3 Click the tool you want to use (see the table on the next page for details)

4 Drag the tool within the white drawing area

 Caution The latest version of Paint edits and saves files only in BMP (bitmap) and PC Paintbrush formats.

Icon	Tool Name	Description
	Free-Form Select	Selects freeform part of the drawing to copy, move, or edit
	Eraser	Erases background color, text, and lines
	Pick Color	Picks up a color from picture for drawing
	Pencil	Draws freeform lines
	Airbrush	Sprays color in a dotted pattern
	Line	Draws straight lines
	Rectangle	Draws rectangles with straight corners (hold down Shift while dragging to get squares)
	Ellipse	Draws circles or ellipses (hold down Shift while dragging to get circles)
	Select	Selects rectangular part of the drawing to copy, move, or edit
	Fill with Color	Fills a closed area with the current color
	Magnifier	Enlarges view of drawing
	Brush	Draws with a brush of varying thickness
	Text	Adds letters and characters
	Curve	Draws curved lines
	Polygon	Draws polygons from connected straight lines
	Rounded Rectangle	Draws rectangles with rounded corners (hold down Shift while dragging to get rounded square)

To fill a shape with color

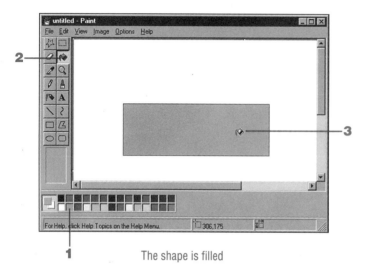

The shape is filled

1. Click a color

2. Click the Fill with Color tool

3. Click inside the shape

Tip You can fill a shape again with a different color.

To use the brush

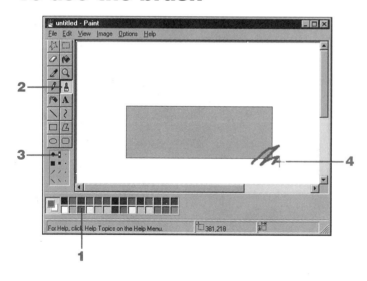

1. Click a color

2. Click the Brush tool

3. Click a Brush shape

4. Drag the tool in the drawing area

To draw a line

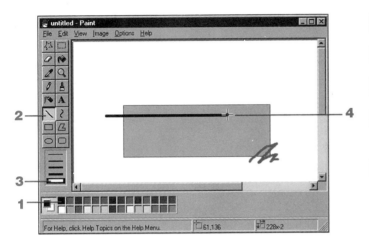

1 Click a color

2 Click the Line tool

3 Click a line width

4 Drag the tool in the drawing area

5 Release to draw the line

To erase part of a drawing

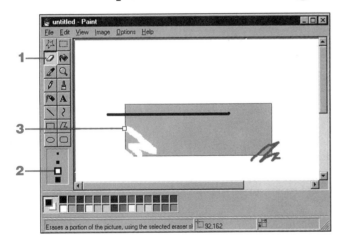

1 Click the Eraser tool

2 Click an Eraser size

3 Drag the Eraser in the drawing area

13

To insert text

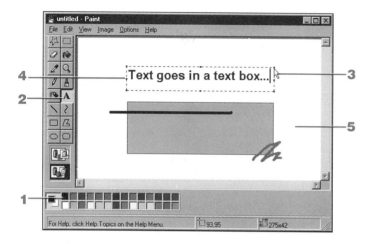

1 Click a color

2 Click the Text tool

3 Drag a text box

4 Type the desired text

5 Click outside of the text box

To erase a selected area

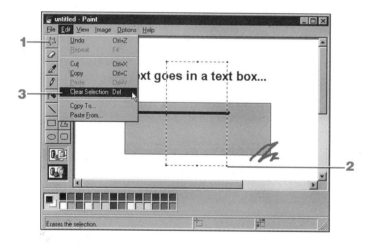

1 Click a selection tool

2 Drag around the area to clear

3 Choose Edit, Clear Selection or press Del

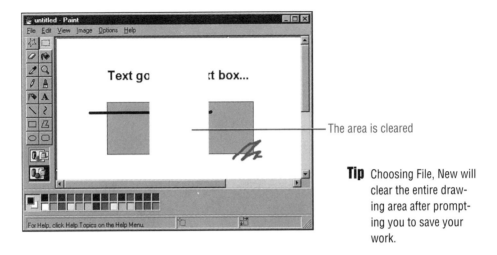

The area is cleared

Tip Choosing File, New will clear the entire drawing area after prompting you to save your work.

Note

Clearing an area is not an irreversible action. Immediately choose Edit, Undo to restore the cleared area to its previous state.

To print a file

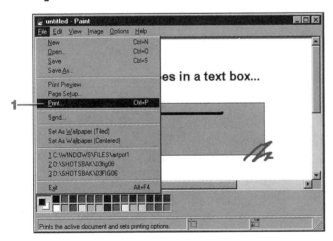

1 Choose File, Print

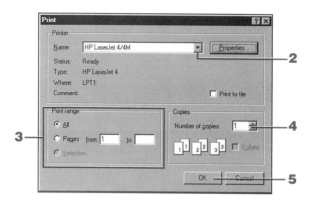

2 Select a printer, if necessary

3 Select the print range

4 Select the number of copies to print

5 Click OK

Tip Click Properties to change paper size, orientation, and paper source.

To save a file

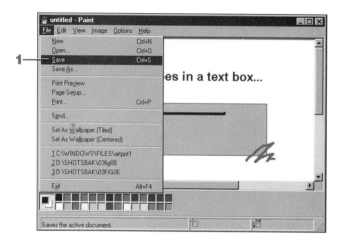

1 Choose File, Save (follow steps 2-7 below if you have not saved this file before)

Tip To open an existing Paint file, choose File, Open and select the file you want to open.

2 Click the drop-down button

3 Click a drive icon or Network Neighborhood

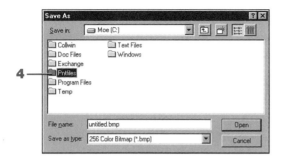

4 Double-click a destination folder— keep repeating until you find the right folder

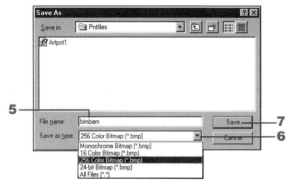

5 Type a file name

6 Select a file type, if desired

7 Click Save

Using WordPad

WordPad is a true word processor that can apply formatting to characters and the page. WordPad saves files in a format that can be read by Microsoft Word for Windows.

To use WordPad

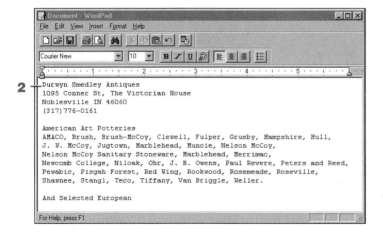

1 Choose Start, Programs, Accessories, WordPad

2 Enter and edit text as desired

Tip If you make a mistake while editing, immediately choose Edit, Undo to reverse the last action.

To copy and paste text

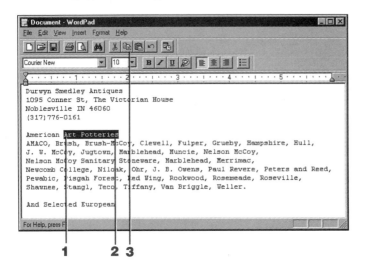

1 Click the starting point

2 Drag to the end of the desired text

3 Click the Copy button

Tip To delete marked text, click the Cut button. The deleted text may be pasted elsewhere if desired.

Note

WordPad saves files in Word for Windows (DOC), Rich Text (RTF), and text (TXT) formats. WordPad will edit and save existing Write (WRI) files but will not create new ones.

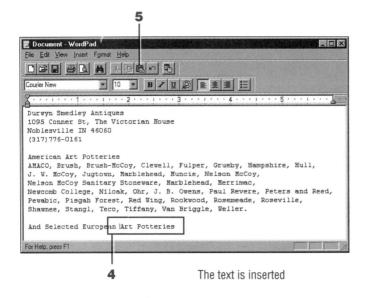

4 Click at the location where you want to insert text

Click the Paste button

The text is inserted

To select text

1 Click the starting point

2 Drag to the end of the desired text

Note

After you select text and apply formatting, the text remains selected. Figure in the following sections has been deselected so that you can see the formatting.

To boldface selected text

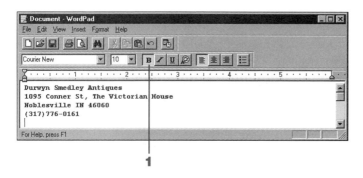

1 Click the Bold button

To italicize selected text

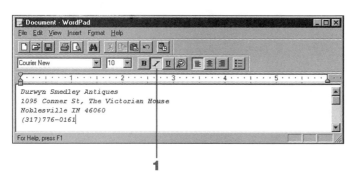

1 Click the Italic button

To underline selected text

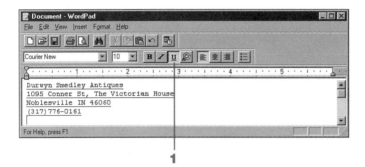

1 Click the Underline button

To change the color of selected text

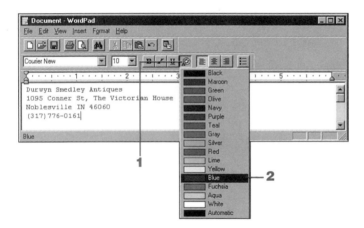

1 Click the Color button

2 Click a color

To left-align selected text

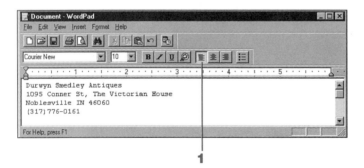

1 Click the Align Left button

To center selected text

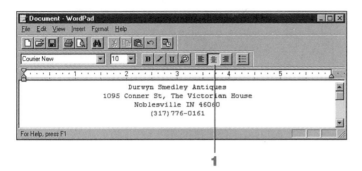

1 Click the Center button

To right-align selected text

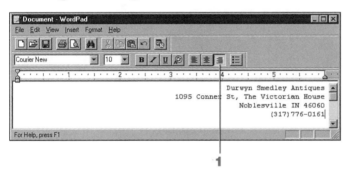

1 Click the Right Align button

To change the font of selected text

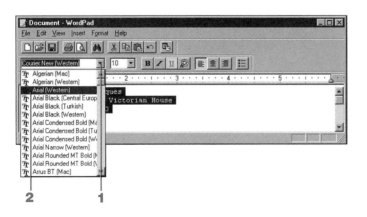

1 Click the Font drop-down button

2 Click a font

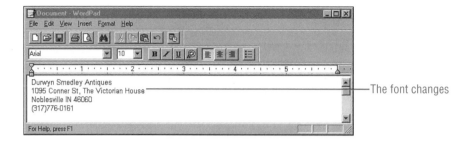
The font changes

To change the font size of selected text

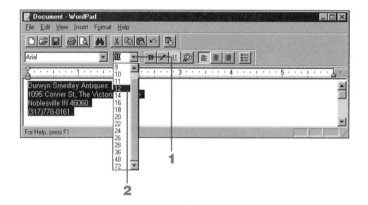

1 Click the Font Size drop-down button

2 Click a font size

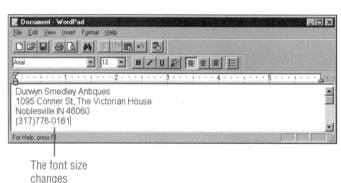

The font size changes

To insert a bullet

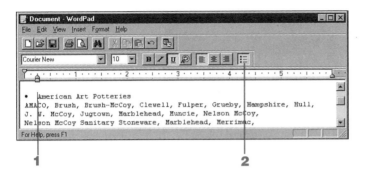

1 Click the insertion point

2 Click the Bullets button

3 When you are done inserting bullets, click the Bullets button again

To find text

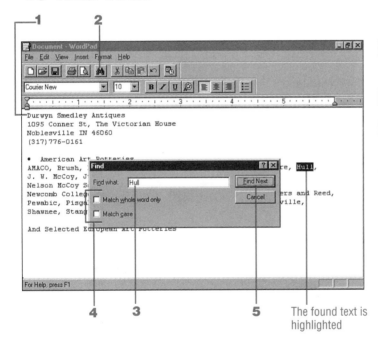

1 Click at the beginning of the document

2 Click the Find button

3 Type the text to search for

4 Click search options, if desired

5 Click Find Next until you find the text you want

6 Click Cancel

The found text is highlighted

Note

Click Find Next to find the next occurrence of the text. If you have not selected the Match Whole Word Only option, WordPad will continue finding the text even if it is embedded in another word.

Tip A message box informs you if no match is found.

To print a file

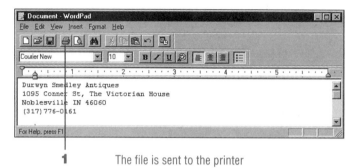

1 Click the Print button

1 The file is sent to the printer

Note

Because there are no printing options to select, clicking the Print button immediately sends the file to the printer. A dialog box offers you a Cancel command button, but most memo-length files are sent to the printer so quickly that they cannot be canceled.

To save a file

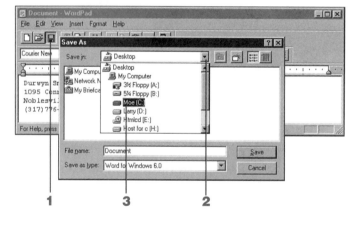

1 Click the Save button

2 If you have not saved the file before, click the drop-down button

3 Click a drive icon or Network Neighborhood

Tip To open an existing text file with WordPad, choose File, Open and select the file you want to open.

1   **3**   **2**

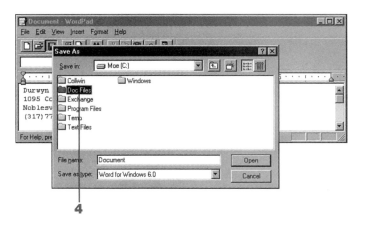

4 Double-click a destination folder—repeat as necessary to get to the right folder

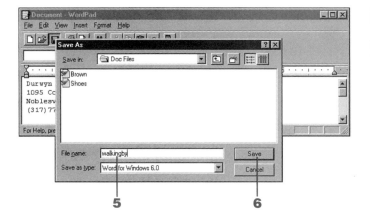

5 Type a file name

6 Click Save

Note

Windows 95 allows you to use long file names. You are not limited to eight-character file names and three-character extensions. You may include spaces in file names.

Starting and Exiting Windows

Typically, Windows starts when you boot your computer. If your computer is not configured in this manner, you can start Windows from the system's command prompt. Windows can be started from any directory if the system's path includes the \WINDOWS folder.

To start Windows

1 At the DOS prompt, type WIN

2 Press Enter

1 Windows opens to the desktop

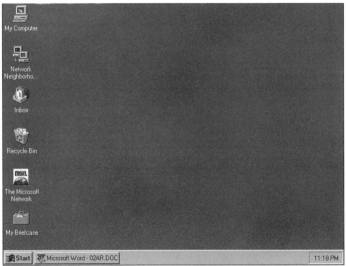

Note

If you have programs in the STARTUP folder, they will run after the desktop opens. Many people keep a copy of the Inbox icon in the STARTUP folder so that they can check for new e-mail messages when they begin work.

To exit Windows

1 Click Start

2 Click Shut Down

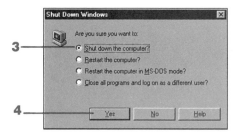

3 Select Shut Down the
Computer if necessary

4 Click Yes

Tip Be sure to use
the Shut Down
command to exit
Windows before
turning off your
computer.

Note

The Shut Down Windows dialog box offers options to the
user. You can restart the computer and reload Windows, or
restart the computer in MS-DOS mode only. Network users
can close all programs and log on again.

Parts of the Windows Screen

The desktop is the background on which windows and icons are displayed. The user starts most Windows tasks from the desktop. Individual windows have the same basic components as the desktop.

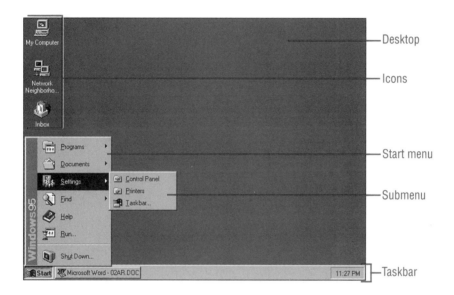

— Desktop

— Icons

— Start menu

— Submenu

— Taskbar

Mouse Operations

The mouse is a pointing device for manipulating windows, menus, and commands, and selecting text and graphics.

To point and click

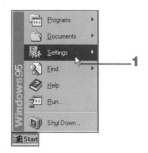

1 Position the mouse pointer on the item (point)

29

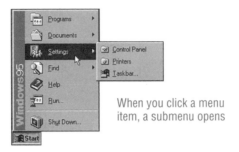

When you click a menu
item, a submenu opens

2 Quickly press and
release the left
mouse button (click)

To double-click

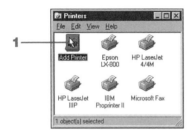

1 Position the mouse
pointer on the item
(point)

2 Quickly press and
release the left
mouse button twice
(double-click)

To move a window by dragging

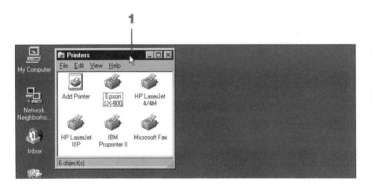

1 Position the mouse
pointer on the title bar

2 Press and hold the
left mouse button

3 Drag the item to the
desired position

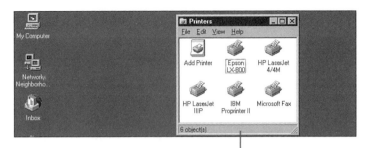

4 Release the mouse button

The window moves to the new location

Tip You can also move icons by dragging.

To resize a window by dragging

The pointer changes to a double-headed arrow

1 Position the mouse pointer on any corner or side

2 Press and hold the left mouse button

3 Drag the item to the desired size

4 Release the mouse button

The enlarged window

Tip You can either enlarge or reduce the size of a window by dragging.

Arranging Icons

You can arrange a window's icons so that they are evenly spaced in the window. Menu selections allow you to display icons in different ways.

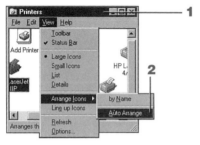

The icons move into a grid pattern

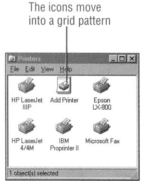

1 Click the title bar to select the window

2 Choose View, Arrange Icons, Auto Arrange

Tip The View menu contains commands to manually or automatically display icons in alphanumeric order.

Opening a Window or Application

An application is a program that performs tasks. A window is a rectangular frame in which you view applications, files, or icons. Applications and files are organized in groups. A group is indicated by a folder icon.

To open an application or window from a menu

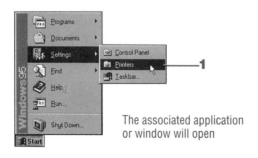

The associated application or window will open

1 Click the folder name

To open an application or window from a window

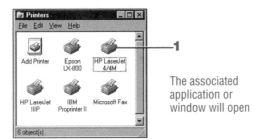

1 Double-click the icon

The associated application or window will open

Closing a Window

Close unneeded windows and reopen them when they are needed again.

You can also double-click the icon in this corner to close the window

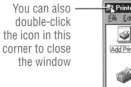 

1 Click the Close button

Selecting a Window

Only one window is active at a given time. You can designate the active window to quickly switch from application to application or window to window.

Tip The active window usually has a different color or shading from the other windows.

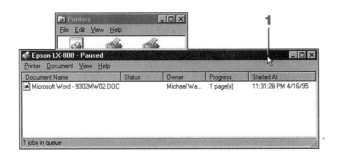

1 Click the title bar of the window; the active window is moved to the foreground of the desktop

Minimizing and Maximizing Windows

You can minimize a window (reduce it to an icon) or maximize a window (enlarge it to fill the entire screen). Restoring returns a window to the size that it was immediately before it was minimized or maximized.

To minimize a window

The window is reduced to an icon in the Taskbar

1 Click the Minimize button

Tip To restore a minimized window, click its button on the Taskbar.

To maximize a window

The window expands to fill the screen

1 Click the Maximize button

To restore a maximized window

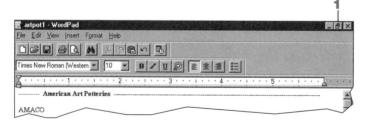

The window resumes its previous size

1 Click the Restore button

Tip The window also may be restored to its previous size by double-clicking the title bar.

Using Windows Communications Accessories

Communications accessories are small applications that enable your computer to act as a terminal to a remote computer, or function as a phone dialer.

To start and close an accessory program

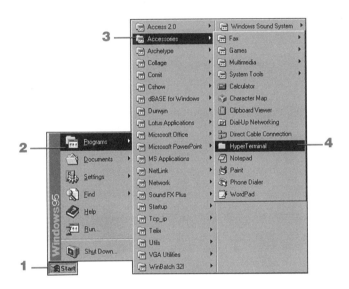

1 Click Start

2 Click Programs

3 Click Accessories

4 Click the name of the program you want

5 When you're finished with the accessory program, click the Close button

Using HyperTerminal

HyperTerminal functions as a terminal program to access online sevices. Properties used for accessing a specific service can be saved as a "connection."

To start HyperTerminal

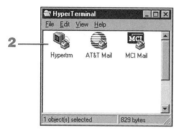

1 Choose Start, Programs, Accessories, HyperTerminal

2 Double-click the HyperTerminal icon

To create a new connection

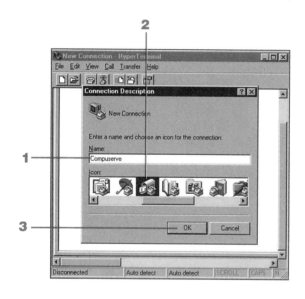

1 Type a connection name

2 Select an icon, if desired

3 Click OK

4 Select the country code, if necessary

5 Type the area code, if necessary

6 Type the phone number

7 Select a modem or direct connection, if necessary

8 Click OK

36

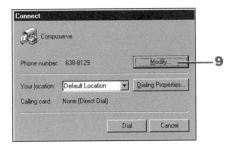

9 Click Modify to modify connection properties

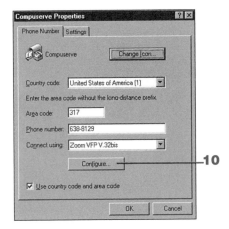

10 Click Configure to change the modem configuration, if necessary (the next four figures show typical modem settings that can be changed with this option)

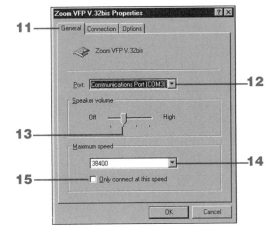

11 Click the General tab, if necessary

12 Select a port

13 Set the speaker volume, if necessary

14 Select the maximum connection speed

15 Click to connect only at maximum speed, if desired

Note

It is usually best not to force HyperTerminal to use only the maximum speed. This allows HyperTerminal to negotiate a lower speed if the remote computer requires it. Set the maximum speed to the baud rate that HyperTerminal will use without displaying error messages.

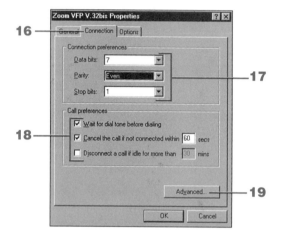

16 Click the Connection tab

17 Select the number of data bits, parity, and the number of stop bits

18 Select your calling preferences

19 Click Advanced to change additional settings, if desired

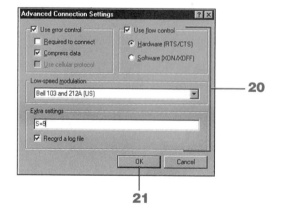

20 Change error control, flow control, and other settings as desired

21 Click OK

Note

The Extra settings text box allows you to enter additional modem initialization strings. These will override any default initialization strings.

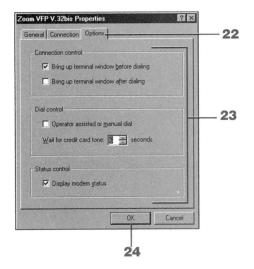

22 Click the Options tab

23 Change connection, status, and dial control settings, if desired

24 Click OK to return to setting up the connection

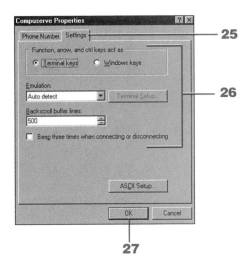

25 Click the Settings tab to change the connection settings, if desired

26 Change the settings as necessary

27 Click OK

Note

Most connections work well with terminal emulation set to Auto Detect. If text or graphics do not display correctly, it may be necessary to set emulation to a specific terminal type that is compatible with the remote computer.

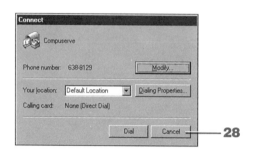

28 Click Cancel to close the connection setup process

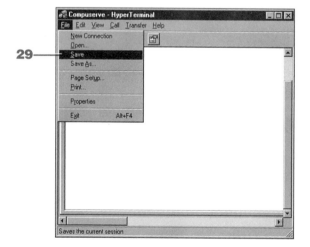

29 Choose File, Save

Tip The typical file saving procedure is not used by HyperTerminal. The new connection file is stored in the default folder using the file name you specified.

Note

After a connection is configured, its icon appears in the
HyperTerminal window. The window can hold many different connection icons that you can run by double-clicking.

To use a connection

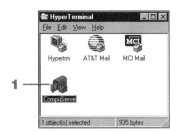

1 Double-click a
connection icon

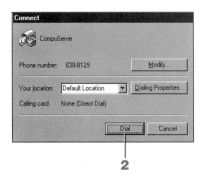

2 Click Dial

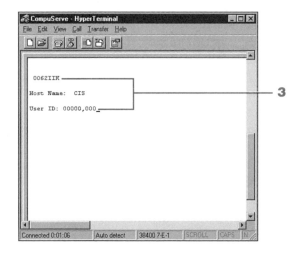

3 Enter login information as necessary

Note

The HyperTerminal font and window may be very small. Use the View, Font command to increase the font size. This will increase both the font size and window size as shown in this example.

To upload a file

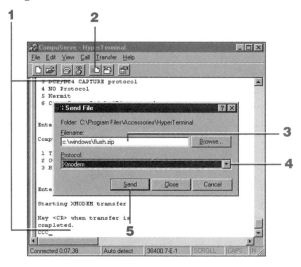

1 Prepare the remote system for the file transfer

2 Click the Send button

3 Type the file name or click Browse and find the desired file

4 Select a protocol

5 Click Send

The file is transferred

Caution The remote system and your computer must both use the same protocol during a file transfer.

To download a file

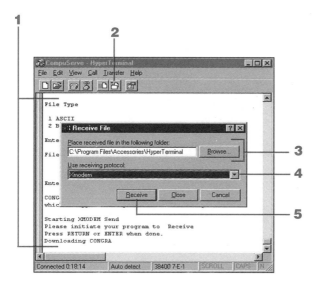

The file is transferred

1 Prepare the remote system for the file transfer

2 Click the Receive button

3 Type or browse for a destination directory

4 Select a protocol

5 Click Receive

Tip If you do not know the full path of the destination directory, you can find it by using the Browse button.

6 If the protocol you are using does not support file name transmission, type a file name

7 Click OK

Caution The remote system and your computer must both use the same protocol during a file transfer.

To capture text from the HyperTerminal window

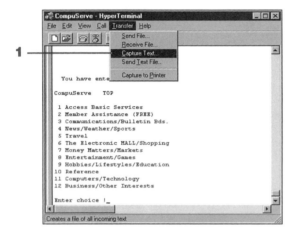

1 Choose Transfer, Capture Text

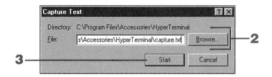

2 Type the path and name of the new capture file

3 Click Start

Tip If you do not know the full path for the capture file, you can find it by using the Browse button.

To stop text capture

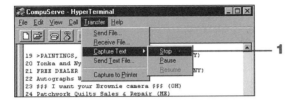

1 Choose Transfer,
Capture Text, Stop

Note

The capture can be paused or resumed while the file is open.
Choose the Pause or Resume command from the Transfer,
Capture Text menu.

To disconnect from the remote system

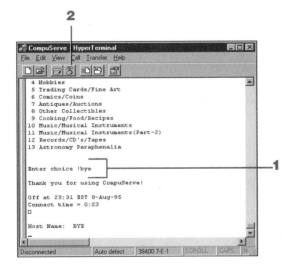

1 Prepare the
remote system for
disconnection

2 Click the Disconnect
button, if necessary

Caution Always prepare the remote system for
disconnection before you disconnect.
Failing to do so may leave an open
connection at the remote system.

Using Phone Dialer

You can enter and dial phone numbers with the Phone Dialer. Frequently used numbers may be assigned to Speed Dial buttons.

To use Phone Dialer

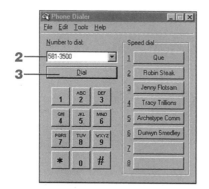

1 Choose Start, Programs, Accessories, Phone Dialer

2 Type the phone number you want to call

3 Click Dial

Note

Use the Speed Dial buttons to quickly dial often-used numbers. Click an unnamed Speed Dial button to assign a name and number to it.

Tip Many people run Phone Dialer automatically from the Startup group.

Caution To use Phone Dialer, your modem must be connected to a phone line that is not already in use. If you are using an external modem, it must be connected to a power source and turned on.

Using the Microsoft Mail Postoffice

The Microsoft Mail Administration utility allows you to create a new Postoffice or set the properties of an existing one for the sending and receiving of mail messages.

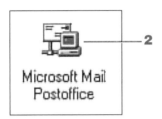

— 2

1 Choose Start, Settings, Control Panel

2 Double-click the Microsoft Mail Postoffice icon

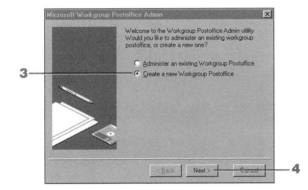

3 —

— 4

3 Click Create a new Workgroup Postoffice

4 Click Next

Tip The Workgroup Postoffice folder must exist before you can create the Workgroup Postoffice.

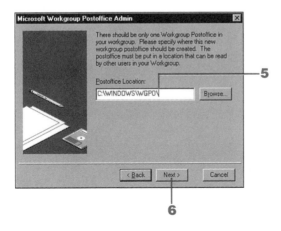

— 5

6

5 Enter a path for the new location

6 Click Next

47

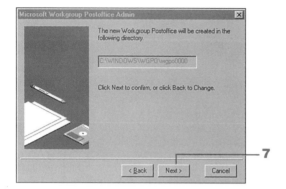

7 Click Next

8 Click OK to continue

9 Enter Administrator Account details

10 Click OK

11 Click OK to continue

Using the Windows Control Panel

The Control Panel lets you change the setup of your computer and many of its devices. For example, you can control how your display looks, install new equipment (see "Equipment: Installation and Setup" for details), or change how the Taskbar works. For each set of steps in this section, you work from the Control Panel.

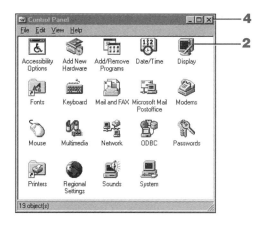

1 Choose Start, Settings, Control Panel

2 Double-click the item you want to change

3 Change settings as desired

4 Click the Close button to close the Control Panel

Installing and Uninstalling Application Programs

The program you want to install or uninstall should come with directions for installing or uninstalling. The following steps are those you generally follow to get ready for the setup process.

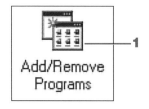

1 Double-click the Add/Remove Programs icon in the Control Panel window

Note

If you are installing a program from CD-ROM, Windows
may automatically begin the installation when you insert the
CD-ROM.

2 Click the
Install/ Uninstall
tab if
necessary

3 Click Install

Note

Programs that can be automatically uninstalled will appear in
the lower half of this dialmog box. Click Remove to proceed
with this process.

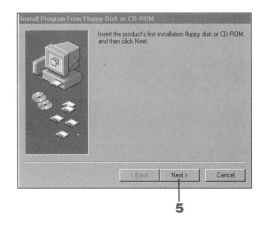

4 Insert the disk or
CD-ROM containing
the program

5 Click Next

Tip There may be a short
delay while Windows
accesses the disk.

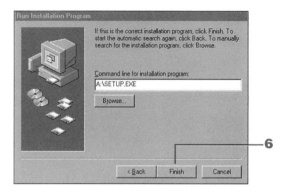

6 Click Finish

7 When the installation starts, follow the program's instructions to install or uninstall

Tip Most programs install and uninstall from a file called Install.exe or Setup.exe. If you're not sure how to install or uninstall your program, click the Browse button at step 6 above and look for a file with one of these names.

Adding and Removing Windows Components

Depending on the amount of disk space you have available and the kind of things you do with your computer, you may decide to add or remove some parts of Windows. For example, if you are low on disk space, consider removing accessories or games that you don't use.

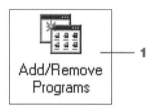

1 Double-click the Add/Remove Programs icon in the Control Panel window

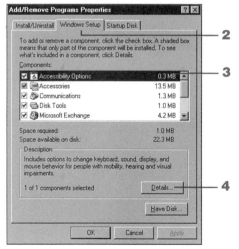

2 Click the Windows Setup tab

3 Click the component you want to install/uninstall

4 Click Details

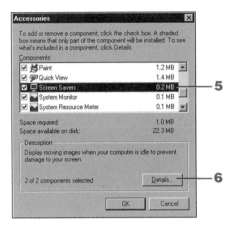

5 Click the specific parts you want to install/uninstall

6 Click Details if necessary

Note

If a check box is checked, the component(s) will be installed.
If a check box is blank, the component(s) will be uninstalled.

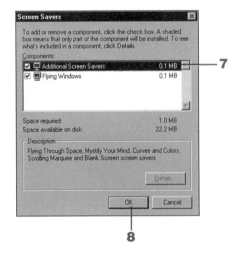

7 Click the components you want to install/uninstall

8 Click OK

9 Click OK again to continue

Changing the Look of the Windows Desktop

To a large degree, you can control how the Windows screen looks—changing colors, adding screen savers, and so on. The best method is to experiment until you find a setup that suits you. Keep in mind, though, that wallpaper, patterns, screen savers, and so on use memory and disk space. You may find that the more options you use, the more Windows' performance degrades.

To access any of the display options, you begin with the Display Properties dialog box. After you change settings as desired, don't forget to close the Control Panel.

Tip As you get things set up the way you like in the Display Properties dialog box, click Apply rather than waiting to click OK when you're completely done.

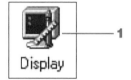

1 Double-click the Display icon in the Windows Control Panel

To add a background pattern

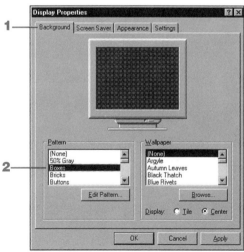

1 Click the Background tab if necessary

2 Select a pattern

Tip Click Edit Pattern to run the Pattern Editor. Click pixels as desired to change the pattern. The Sample window shows how the results will look; when you get something you like, type a Name for it and choose Add to save it. Then choose Done.

Note

Windows resources are used to display wallpaper and background patterns. When these features are disabled, screens display at a faster rate.

To set up wallpaper

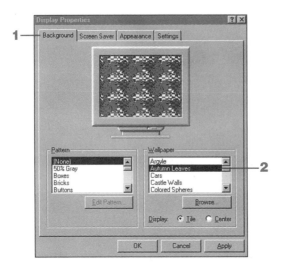

1 Click the Background tab if necessary

2 Select a wallpaper pattern

Tip Click Browse to locate other .BMP files to use as wallpaper.

Tip Wallpaper will obscure any pattern in use. Don't use wallpaper and a pattern at the same time.

To turn the screen saver on or off

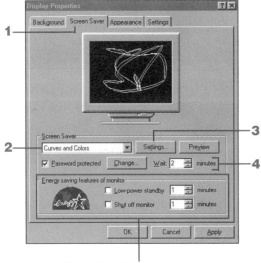

If you do not have an energy-saving monitor, these features will not appear

1 Click the Screen Saver tab

2 Select the screen saver you want

3 Click to change screen saver options, if desired

4 Select the time period before activation

Tip Click Preview to see a full screen view of the current screen saver.

To change colors and fonts

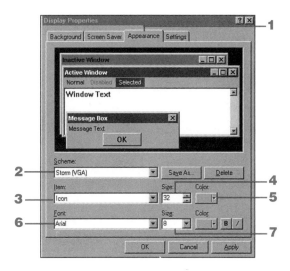

1 Click the Appearance tab

2 Select a color scheme to use

3 Click a screen item whose color you want to change

4 To enlarge or reduce the size of the item (if available), change this setting

5 Select an item color, if available

6 If desired, select a different font

7 If desired, change the font size

Note

To create custom colors, click Color, then Other. Click a color to start with, and then click in the color spectrum, use the vertical slider bar, or adjust numbers for Hue, Saturation, etc. When you get something you like, click Add to Custom Colors, click the Color in the Custom Colors section, and click OK.

Note

It is best to make appearance changes and save the changes as a new color scheme. Click Save As to start the file saving process. If you are not happy with the new color scheme, you can reload one of Windows' standard schemes.

Tip When a screen item is selected, only relevant appearance features are available for modification.

To change the display settings

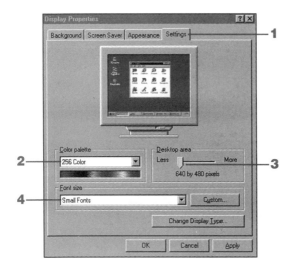

1 Click the Settings tab

2 Select the color palette you want to use

3 Select the resolution you want—640x480, 800x600, and so on

4 Select the display font size, if desired

Caution DO NOT experiment with the Change Display Type option! If you don't know what you're doing, you can permanently damage your monitor.

Adding Fonts

New fonts are added from the Fonts window. The fonts you add are then available to all programs that use selectable fonts.

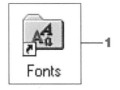

1 Double-click the Fonts icon in the Control Panel window

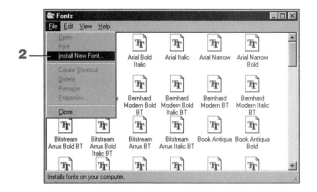

2 Choose File, Install New Font

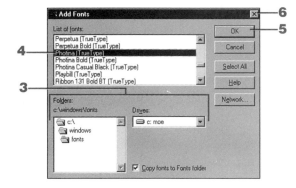

3 Specify the drive and folder where the font files are stored

4 Select a font to install

5 Click OK

6 Click the Close button

7 Click the Close button in the Fonts window

Setting Up Passwords for Security

You can configure security features to password-protect your computer. Options vary, depending on whether you're working on a standalone PC or are part of a network or workgroup.

To add passwords on a networked system

1 Double-click the Passwords icon in the Control Panel

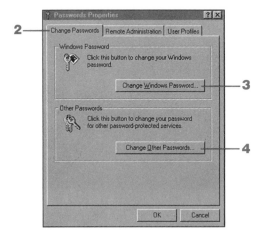

2 Click the Change Passwords tab, if necessary

3 Click this option if you want to change the Windows password

4 Click this option if you want to change the password for other services

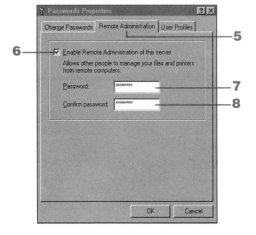

5 Click the Remote Administration tab

6 Click to enable remote administration

7 Enter the password

8 Enter the same password again to confirm

Note

Remote administration allows others in your workgroup to use your password-protected files and printers. You must give the password to other workgroup users.

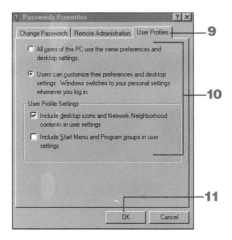

9 Click the User Profiles tab

10 Select profile settings

11 Click OK

Note

After password settings are configured, you must reboot the computer before passwords are enabled. When Windows loads, a dialog box shows your user name and prompts for the password. Enter the password and click OK to continue loading Windows.

Tip Passwords should be used only for significant security needs. Passwords are merely a nuisance if not required.

Setting the Date, Time, and Time Zone

The Date and Time settings allow you to change the date, time zone, and time of your computer's clock. This feature controls the clock that appears at the right end of the Taskbar, and allows for differences in time zones if you're faxing or e-mailing information to another time zone. Note that regional settings affect the display of the system clock. See the section "Changing the Regional Settings" for details.

To set the date or time

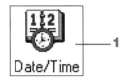

1 Double-click the Date/Time icon in the Control Panel

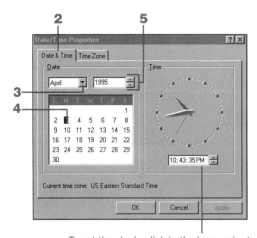

2 Click the Date & Time tab if necessary

3 Select the month

4 Select the day

5 Select the year

To set the clock, click in the hour, minute, or seconds part of the display; then type the correct time or click the up-arrow or down-arrow to change the setting

To set the time zone

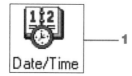

1 Double-click the Date/Time icon in the Control Panel

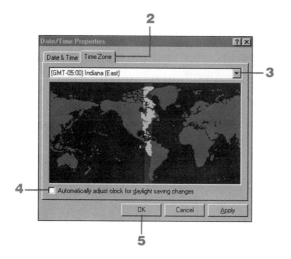

2 Click the Time Zone tab

3 Select the time zone

4 If your area observes Daylight Savings, click this option

5 Click OK

Note

To ensure correct tracking of Daylight Savings time, make sure that the correct time zone is selected for your area.

Changing the Regional Settings

Regional settings control date, number, and currency formats for a specified locale. In London, for example, dates may be displayed as 31 December 1995 rather than December 31, 1995.

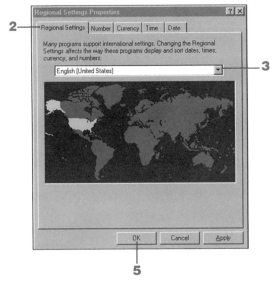

1 Double-click the Regional Settings icon in the Control Panel

2 Click the Regional Settings tab, if necessary

3 Select the appropriate region

4 Specify formats (as described in the next few sections)

5 Click OK

To change the number format

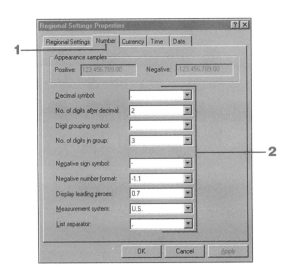

1 Click the Number tab

2 Select or enter the appropriate formats to use when displaying numbers

To change the currency format

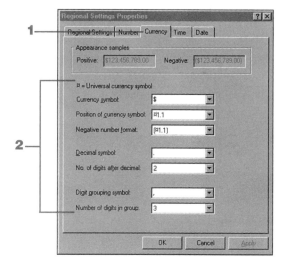

1 Click the Currency tab

2 Select or enter the appropriate formats to use when displaying currency information

To change the time format

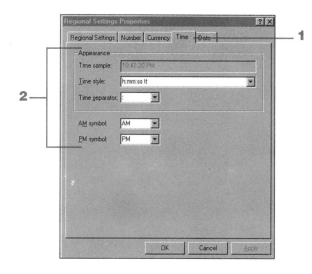

1 Click the Time tab

2 Select the desired time appearance

To change the date format

1 Click the Date tab

2 Select the short date style

3 Select the date separator

4 Select the long date style

Note

Regional settings cannot be used to set the system date and time. Double-click the Date/Time icon in the Control Panel to set the date and time.

Assigning Sounds to System Events

By default, Windows assigns certain sounds to various system events (starting Windows, exiting Windows, etc.). You can change the sounds to suit you, and even save groups of sounds as sound schemes.

1 Double-click the Sounds icon in the Control Panel

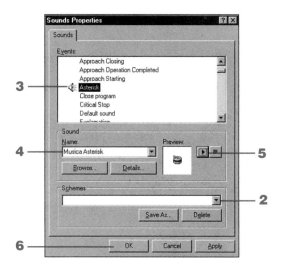

2 Select a Sound Scheme

3 Select an event

4 Select a sound to assign to the event

5 Click to preview sound

6 Click OK

Note

Many users find that assigned sounds are more annoying than useful. Limit the current sound scheme to those sounds that serve a purpose, such as warning you that an error has occurred.

Managing Folders

Folders are used to organize the contents of the desktop. They can contain programs, files, and other folders.

To create a folder

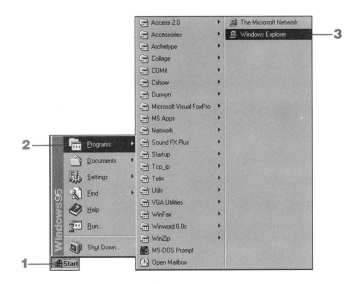

1 Click Start

2 Click Programs

3 Click Windows Explorer

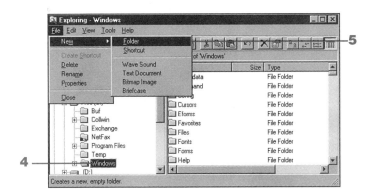

4 Click the drive or folder where you want to create the new folder

5 Choose File, New, Folder

Tip A folder serves the same function as a directory found in previous versions of Windows.

67

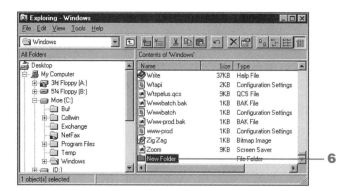

6 Type a new name next to the folder icon

7 Press Enter

To delete a folder

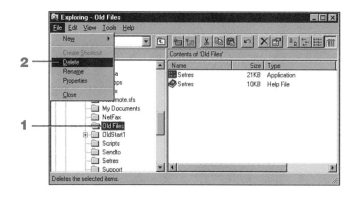

1 Click the folder in the left window

2 Choose File, Delete

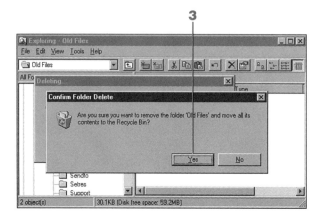

3 Click Yes to delete folder and contents

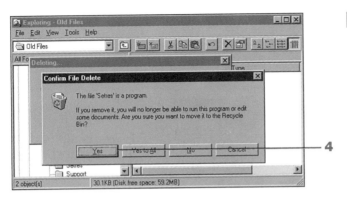

4 If prompted, click Yes

Working with Floppy Disks

You can work with floppy disks as well as hard disks and CD-ROMs in Windows Explorer. Start by opening Explorer; then follow the steps in the next two sections to format or copy disks.

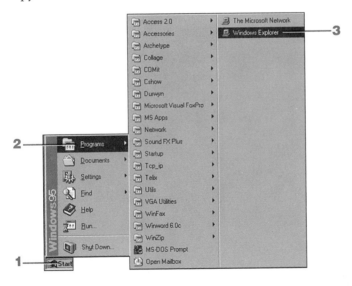

1 Click Start

2 Click Programs

3 Click Windows Explorer

To format a floppy disk

Formatting disks enables them to store files. Disks must be formatted before they can be used.

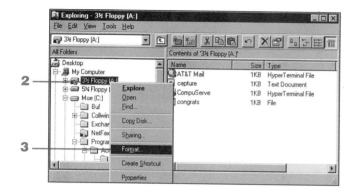

1 Insert a floppy disk

2 In Explorer, right-click the icon for the drive containing the disk

3 Click Format

Tip If the disk has never been formatted, you may be prompted to format it. Click Yes.

4 Select the disk capacity

5 Select the format type

6 Type a disk label, if you want one

7 Select any options you want

8 Click Start

9 Click Close

Copying a Floppy Disk

You can copy disks by using one or two drives.

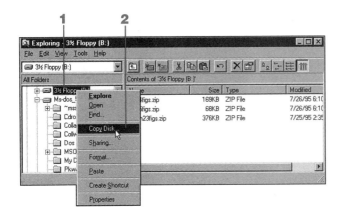

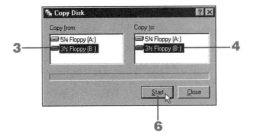

1 In Explorer, right-click the icon for the floppy disk drive

2 Choose Copy Disk

3 Click the icon for the source disk (the disk you want to copy from) in the left box

4 Click the icon for the target disk (the disk you want to copy to) in the right box

5 Insert the source disk in the drive

6 Choose Start

7 When prompted, insert the target disk

8 Choose OK

9 Choose Close

71

Running DOS Commands

DOS internal and external commands are an integral part of Windows 95. These commands may be used to perform DOS-oriented tasks.

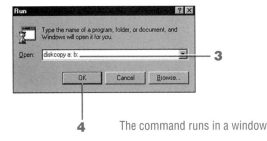

The command runs in a window

1 Click Start

2 Click Run

3 Type a DOS command

4 Click OK

Tip Click the drop-down button to select a previously used command.

Note

You can run any of the "external" DOS commands, such as DISKCOPY or FORMAT, found in the C:\WINDOWS\ COMMAND folder. Commands that are "internal" to the DOS command processor, such as DIR and TYPE, cannot be run.

Note

The MS-DOS Prompt window offers features that are not available from DOS alone. You can control font, memory, and screen properties. You can mark areas of text, cut them to the Clipboard, and paste them into other windows.

Running DOS Applications

Applications can be run from the command line just like DOS commands. If you don't know the command name, you can browse for the name.

1 Click Start

2 Click Run

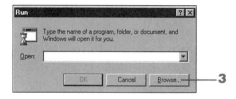

3 Click Browse

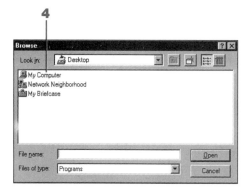

4 Double-click My Computer

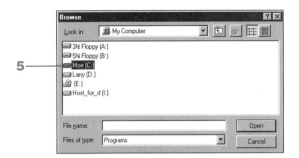

5 Double-click a drive

6 Double-click a folder

7 Click a program

8 Click Open

9 Click OK in the Run dialog box

Tip Windows applications can also be run from the DOS command line.

Editing DOS Application Properties

When a DOS application is run the first time, an additional file is created. This file contains parameters for running the program and can be edited by the user.

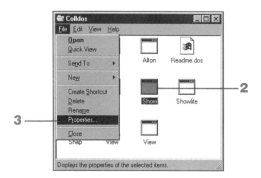

1. **Open the application's folder**

2. **Click the application**

3. **Choose File, Properties**

4. **Change the application's properties (as described in the following sections)**

5. **Click OK**

To configure general properties

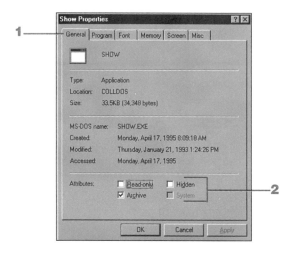

1. **Click the General tab, if necessary**

2. **Change the file's attributes as desired**

Tip A set of properties is equivalent to the PIF file used in previous versions of Windows.

To configure program properties

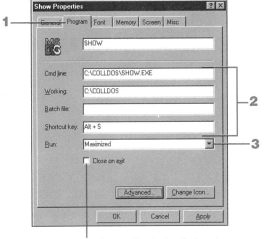

Click here if you want the application's window to close when you exit the program

1 Click the Program tab

2 Edit the parameters as necessary

3 Select the application's window size

Tip Click Change Icon to change the application's icon.

Note

Click Advanced to configure disk cache, memory, and mouse options for the DOS program.

To change the program's default font settings

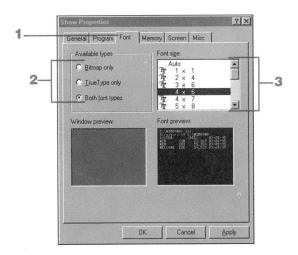

1 Click the Font tab

2 Select a font type

3 Select a font size

Tip TrueType fonts can be resized more easily than bitmap fonts and result in smaller file sizes.

77

To change the memory settings for the program

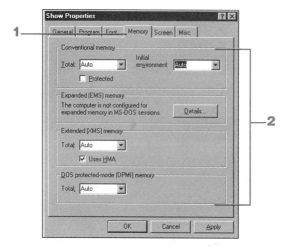

1 Click the Memory tab

2 Specify the appropriate memory amounts

Note

Memory sizes should be specified only when Windows has problems allocating memory. Most programs run properly when all memory amounts are set to Auto.

To change the screen settings

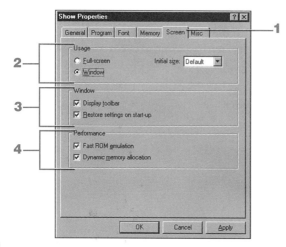

1 Click the Screen tab

2 Select the appropriate screen usage setting

3 Change the window settings as desired

4 Set video ROM and memory features as necessary

To configure miscellaneous application properties

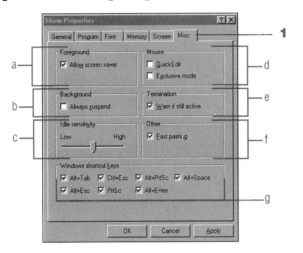

1 Click the Misc tab

2 Choose settings as desired (see table)

Option	Description
a	Click to allow screen saver
b	The Background setting controls the application's ability to run in the background. If the application does not run correctly in the background, or slows the foreground application too much, select Always Suspend.
c	Set idle time sensitivity
d	Select mouse options
e	Click to warn if quitting while active
f	Click for fast pasting
g	Click Windows key combinations to allow (deselect any key combinations that conflict with the application)

Caution Some ill-behaved applications will crash when the screen saver runs. If this happens, deselect Allow Screen Saver.

Adding New Hardware

New devices may be configured by entering the device properties. Some devices have Plug and Play capabilities and configure themselves during this process.

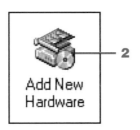

1 Choose Start, Settings, Control Panel

2 Double-click the Add New Hardware icon

3 Click Next

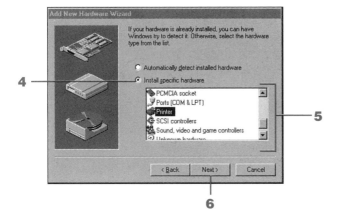

4 Click this option to install specific hardware

5 Select a hardware item to install

6 Click Next

7 Follow additional steps specific to the new device

8 Click OK

81

Creating a Startup Disk

It is important to have a startup disk. This will allow you to start the system if the installed version of Windows is damaged, or the hard disk has errors that prevent booting.

1 Choose Start, Settings, Control Panel

2 Double-click the Add/Remove Programs icon

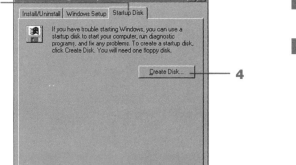

Windows will prepare Startup Disk files

3 Click the Startup Disk tab

4 Click Create Disk

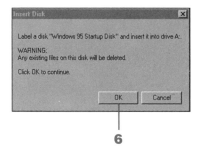

5 Insert a disk in drive A:

6 Click OK

7 Click OK again to continue

Configuring the Keyboard

The keyboard settings control the key repeat speed and the delay time before a key repeats. Keyboard country and language may be designated.

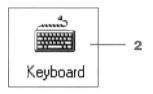

1 Choose Start, Settings, Control Panel

2 Double-click the Keyboard icon

To set the delay and repeat

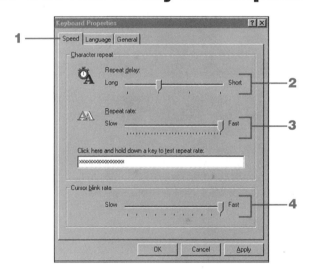

1 Click the Speed tab, if necessary

2 Select the repeat delay

3 Select the repeat rate

4 Select the cursor blink rate

Note

Most accomplished typists will want to set a short repeat delay and a high repeat rate. Adjust these settings to enable maximum typing speed without character overruns.

To change the keyboard language

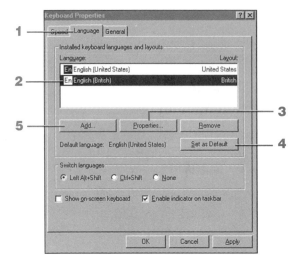

1 Click the Language tab

2 Select a language

3 Click to set keyboard properties, if necessary

4 Click to set this as the default keyboard, if desired

5 Click to add another keyboard language, if desired

To set the keyboard type

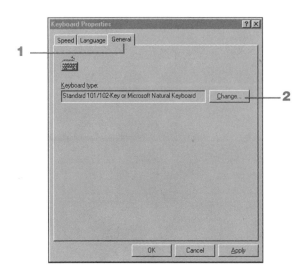

1 Click the General tab

2 Click Change

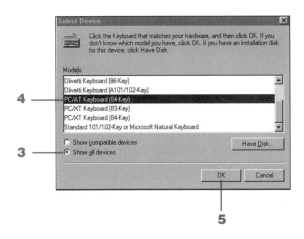

3 Click Show All Devices

4 Select the keyboard type

5 Click OK

6 Click OK again

Configuring Modems

For your modem to work properly, you need to set up the modem properties in Control Panel.

To set modem properties

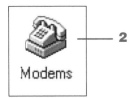

1 Choose Start, Settings, Control Panel

2 Double-click the Modems icon

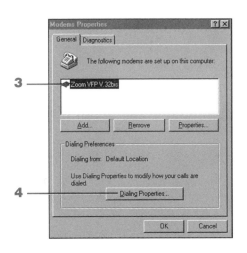

3 Select the modem, if necessary

4 Choose Dialing Properties

Tip Click Add to configure a new modem.

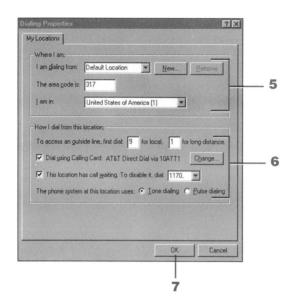

5 Type the location information

6 Specify the dialing information

7 Click OK

8 Click Properties to open a Properties dialog box for the modem you are configuring (see next two figures)

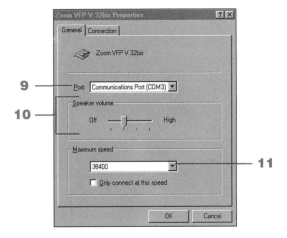

9 Select the port

10 Set the speaker volume

11 Select the maximum speed

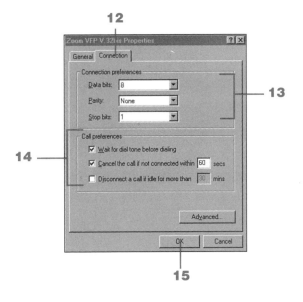

12 Click the Connection tab

13 Set your connection preferences

14 Select your call preferences

15 Click OK to return to the Modems Properties dialog box

Note

Click Advanced if you want to configure error control, flow control, or data compression properties.

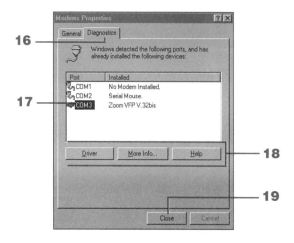

16 Click the Diagnostics tab

17 Select the modem's port

18 Click command buttons as desired for information

19 Click Close

Configuring the Mouse

The characteristics of the mouse, or other pointing device, may be adjusted to suit the user's preferences.

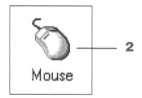

1 Choose Start, Settings, Control Panel

2 Double-click the Mouse icon

To change the button settings

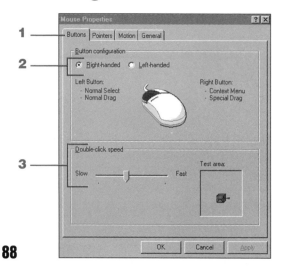

1 Click the Buttons tab, if necessary

2 Select right-handed or left-handed operation

3 Set the double-click speed

Tip Double-click in the Test area until the double-click speed is comfortable for you.

To select a new pointer scheme

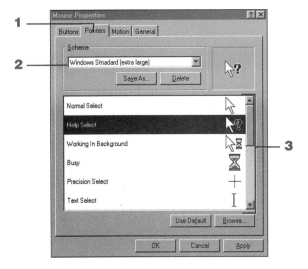

1 Click the Pointers tab

2 Select a scheme

3 Double-click a pointer to browse for a different one, if desired

To configure mouse motion

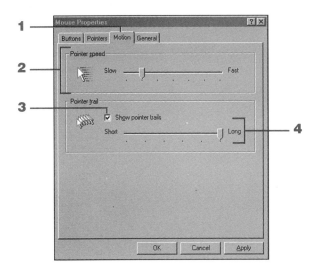

1 Click the Motion tab

2 Set the pointer speed

3 Click to enable pointer trails, if desired

4 Set the length of the pointer trail

To install a different mouse

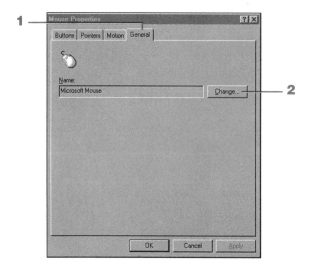

1 Click the General Tab

2 Click Change

3 Click Show All Devices

4 Select the manufacturer

5 Select the model

6 Click OK

7 Click OK again to continue

Configuring Multimedia Properties

Sound properties and other multimedia properties may be changed to suit your equipment and needs. You can also install new multimedia equipment as desired.

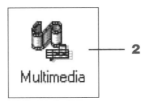

1 Choose Start, Settings, Control Panel

2 Double-click the Multimedia icon

To configure audio properties

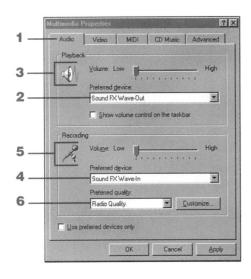

1 Click the Audio tab, if necessary

2 Select the playback device

3 Set playback volume

4 Select the recording device, if any

5 Set the recording volume

6 Select the recording quality

Tip Click Customize to set quality properties.

91

To change the video properties

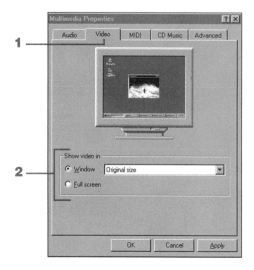

1 Click the Video tab

2 Select the video size

Tip Video may seem choppy if too large a size is selected.

To set up MIDI output

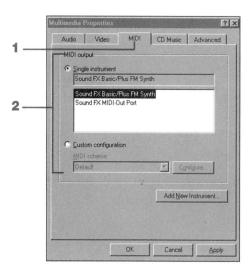

1 Click the MIDI tab

2 Select the desired MIDI instrument

Tip Click Add New Instrument to add a new MIDI device.

Note

Click Custom Configuration to choose a MIDI scheme and configure its properties. This is the method for assigning instruments to channels.

To change the CD-ROM drive volume settings

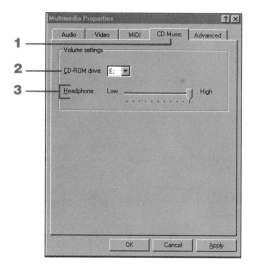

1 Click the CD Music tab

2 Select a CD-ROM drive

3 Set the headphone volume

Tip To ensure that the headphone volume setting is effective, set the CD-ROM drive's volume control to maximum.

To configure advanced properties

1 Click the Advanced tab

2 Select a device

3 Click the Properties button for advanced settings

4 Click OK

Configuring the Network

Certain features allow communications and device-sharing
between members of a workgroup. You can configure these
features to suit your specific workgroup needs.

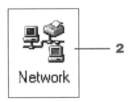

2

1 Choose Start,
   Settings, Control
   Panel

2 Double-click the
   Network icon

To set component properties

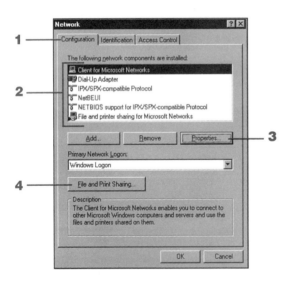

1

2

3

4

1 Click the
   Configuration button

2 Select a network
   component

3 Click the Properties
   button to set
   component properties

4 Click here to set file
   and print sharing
   properties, if
   necessary

To change the identification settings

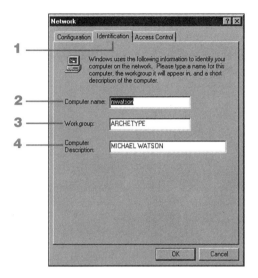

1 Click the Identification tab

2 Type the computer name

3 Type the workgroup name

4 Type the computer description

Tip The computer description is typically the user's full name.

To configure access control for security

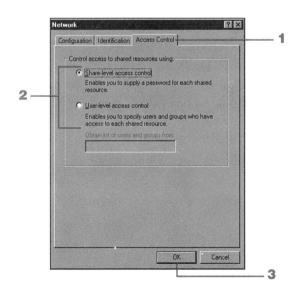

1 Click the Access Control tab

2 Select a level of access control

3 Click OK

Tip You may use user-level control only on NetWare networks or on Microsoft networks running on the Windows NT server.

Configuring Printers

Printer settings, such as paper size and print quality, affect all applications that use the printer.

 —— 2

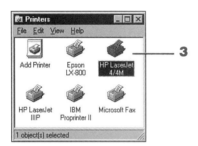 —— 3

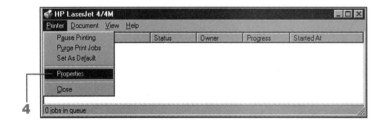

1 Choose Start, Settings, Control Panel

2 Double-click the Printers icon

3 Double-click the printer icon for the printer you want to configure

Tip Double-click the Add Printer icon to install a new printer.

4 Choose Printer, Properties

Tip Your printer may have different properties settings from those shown in the following figures.

To set general printer properties

1 Click the General tab, if necessary

2 Enter a comment, if desired

3 Select a separator page, if desired

Tip Click Print Test Page to confirm that printer operation is correct.

To configure port and timeout settings

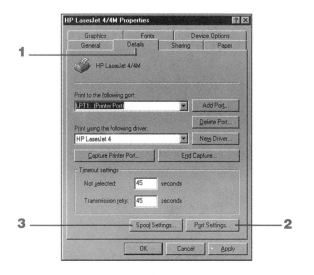

1 Click the Details tab

2 Click to configure the port setting

3 Click to configure spooler properties, if necessary

To allow printer sharing

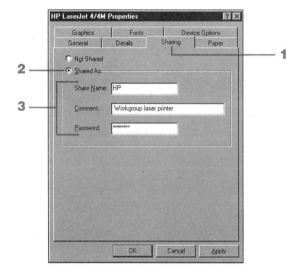

1 Click the Sharing tab

2 Click Shared As to share the printer

3 Enter sharing information

Tip If you enter a password, you will be asked to reenter it for confirmation.

To set up paper size and orientation

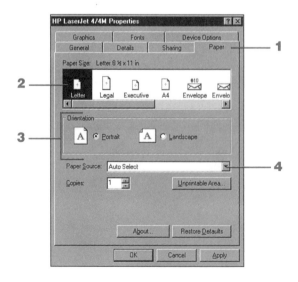

1 Click the Paper tab

2 Select the paper size

3 Select the page orientation

4 Select the paper source

To control print quality for graphics

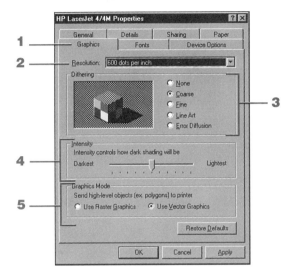

1 Click the Graphics tab

2 Select the print resolution

3 Select the dithering level

4 Set shading density

5 Select a graphics mode

To configure fonts

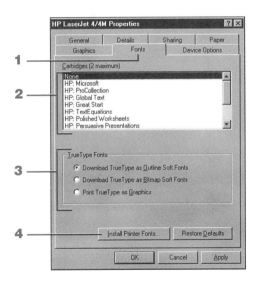

1 Click the Fonts tab

2 Select font cartridges, if available

3 Select a True Type mode

4 Click this button to install fonts, if available

To configure additional device options

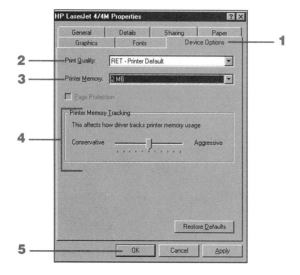

1 Click the Device Options tab

2 Select the print quality

3 Specify the printer memory setting

4 Set memory tracking

5 Click OK

6 Choose Printer, Close to continue

Note

Printer memory tracking optimizes the use of printer memory by Windows. Typically, it should be left at its default setting, unless a specific application has memory problems when printing.

Changing System Properties

You may access the System Properties of physical and virtual devices in your computer. This allows a great degree of flexibility in configuring these devices.

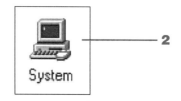

1 Choose Start, Settings, Control Panel

2 Double-click the System icon

To configure devices

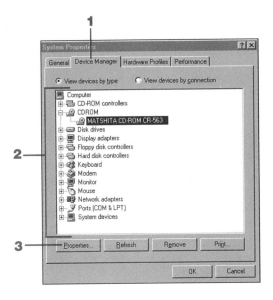

1 Click the Device Manager tab

2 Select the device whose properties you want to change

3 Click the Properties button to configure the computer or device

4 Change settings as necessary

To create new hardware profiles

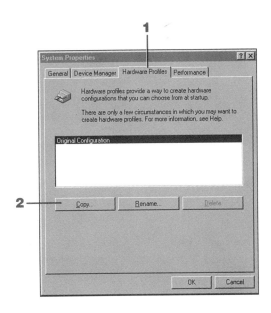

1 Click the Hardware Profiles tab

2 Click Copy to make a duplicate profile

To improve system performance

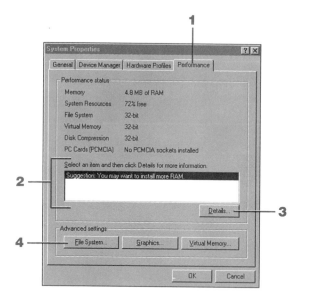

1. **Click the Performance tab**

2. **Select an item**

3. **Click Details for information**

4. **To change the settings, click File System**

Note

You may simply see a dialog box in which Windows states that your system is optimized.

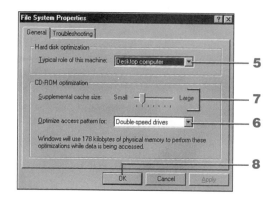

5. **Select the primary machine use**

6. **Select the CD-ROM type**

7. **Set the cache size, if necessary**

8. **Click OK to return to the System Properties dialog box**

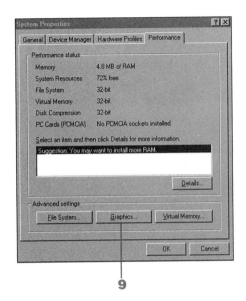

9 Click Graphics if you want to change the graphics settings

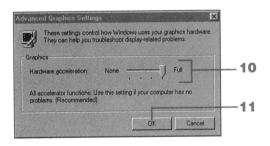

10 Set the hardware acceleration, if necessary

11 Click OK to return to the System Properties dialog box

Note

By default, hardware acceleration is set to maximum. Reduce this setting if your screen does not redraw images correctly.

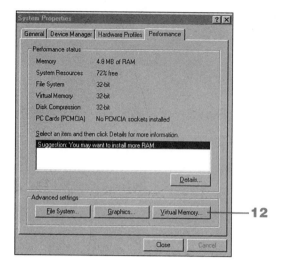

12 Click Virtual Memory if you want to change the memory settings

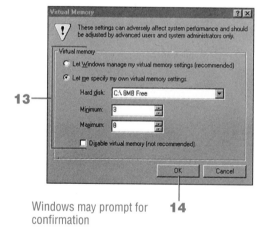

Windows may prompt for confirmation **14**

13 Select virtual memory settings, if desired

14 Click OK

15 Click OK to close the System Properties dialog box

Caution **Windows is efficient with its use of virtual memory.** It is advantageous to let Windows manage the virtual memory settings. Do not change memory settings unless you know what you are doing.

Configuring Accessibility Options

The properties of the keyboard, sound, display, and mouse may be changed to improve accessibility for the hearing- and sight-impaired.

2—

1 Choose Start, Settings, Control Panel

2 Double-click the Accessibility Options icon

3 After changing the accessibility options (as described in the following sections), click OK

To select keyboard options

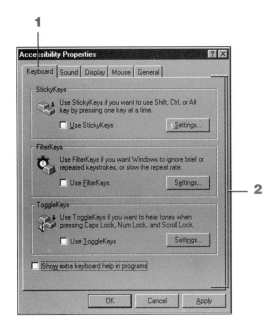

1 Click the Keyboard tab, if necessary

2 Select the desired keyboard options

To choose sound options

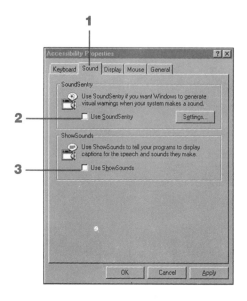

1 Click the Sound tab

2 Click to enable SoundSentry, if desired

3 Click to enable ShowSounds, if desired

Tip Click the Settings buttons to configure each sound option.

To set the display to high contrast

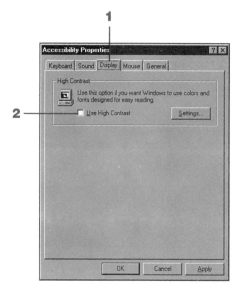

1 Click the Display tab

2 Click the option to enable High Contrast

Tip Click the Settings button to configure the High Contrast option.

To control the mouse with the 10-key pad

1

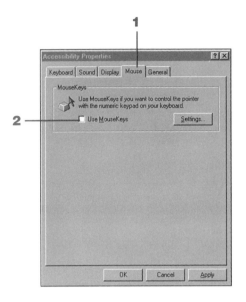

1 Click the Mouse tab

2 Click the option to enable MouseKeys

Tip Click the Settings button to configure the MouseKeys option.

To configure general options

1

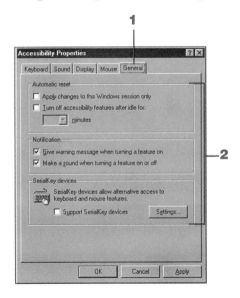

1 Click the General tab

2 Choose the desired settings

107

Using Windows Explorer

Files may be copied, moved, deleted, restored, faxed, mailed, viewed, and opened from the Windows Explorer. Shortcuts may be created to provide quick access to programs or files. For additional information related to Windows Explorer, refer to the "Disk Management" section earlier in this book.

To start Windows Explorer

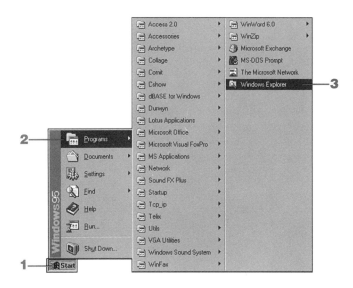

1 Click Start

2 Click Programs

3 Click Windows Explorer

Note

You may run Windows Explorer automatically from the Startup group and use it as your primary working environment. Applications are then run from Windows Explorer by double-clicking the appropriate icon.

To expand the view of a drive

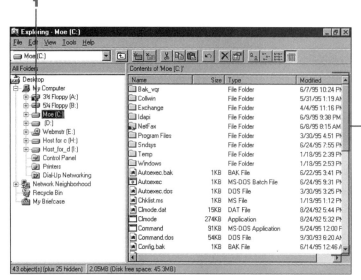

1 Double-click the drive name

This window shows the folders and files of the selected drive

Tip You also can expand a drive by clicking the plus sign next to the drive icon. This updates only the left pane of the window.

The drive view expands

Tip This only expands one level. Drives and folders showing a plus sign contain additional folders. A minus sign indicates that the drive or folder is completely expanded.

To expand the view of a folder

1

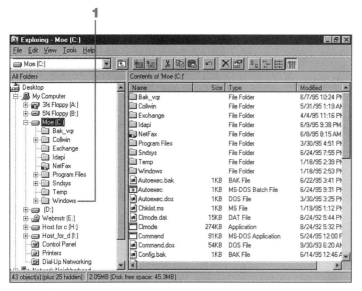

1 Double-click the folder

Tip You also can expand a folder by clicking the plus sign next to the folder icon.

The folder view expands

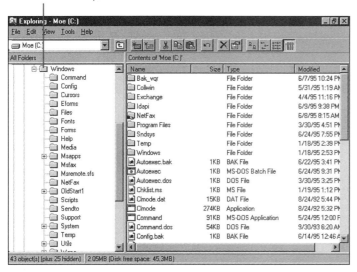

Note

An expanded drive or folder may be closed by clicking the minus sign next to the icon or double-clicking the icon.

To open a file

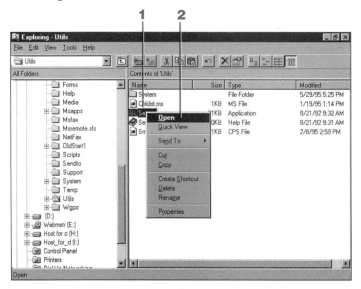

1 Right-click the file

2 Click Open

Tip You also can double-click a file to open it.

The file you selected opens

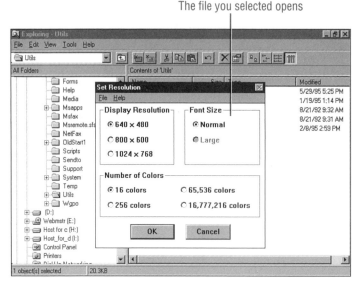

Note

An executable file runs when opened. A document file, such as a spreadsheet, is opened in its associated application. If no associated application is found, Windows prompts you to select an application with which to open the file.

To print a file

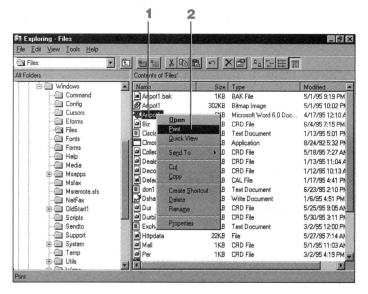

1 Right-click the file

2 Click Print

Tip Only document files display the Print command in the quick menu. Spreadsheets and word processor files are examples of documents.

The file is printed from its associated application

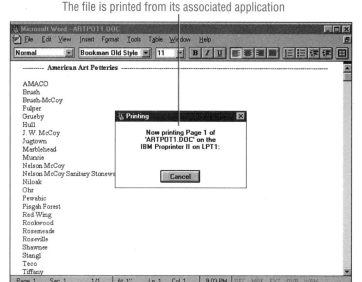

Tip Another quick printing method is to drag the file icon from Explorer to the desktop, and drop it on a printer shortcut icon.

Note

A document file is printed from its associated application. If no associated application is found, Windows prompts you to select an application to open the file and print it.

To preview a file

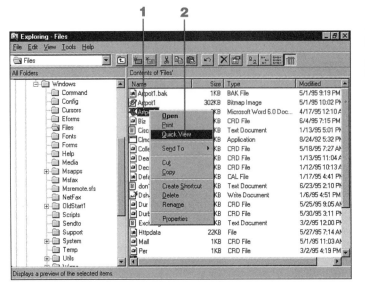

1 Right-click the file

2 Click Quick View

Tip Quick View will display most files containing text or graphics.

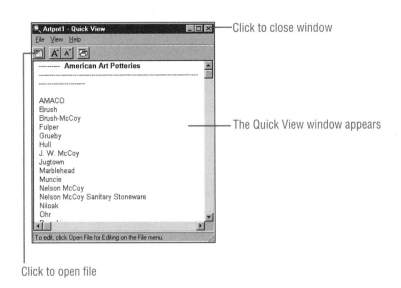

Click to close window

The Quick View window appears

Click to open file

To send a file as a fax

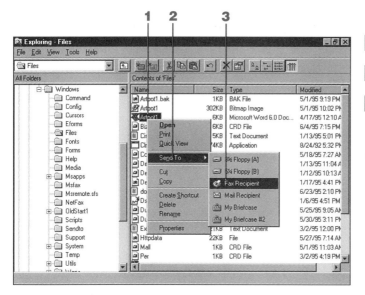

1 Right-click the file

2 Click Send To

3 Click Fax Recipient

Tip The Fax Wizard guides you through all steps required to send the document as a fax.

To send a file as a mail message

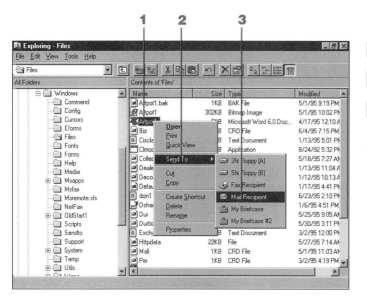

1 Right-click the file

2 Click Send To

3 Click Mail Recipient

Tip Microsoft Exchange opens a new message with the selected file embedded in it. To edit the embedded file, double-click the file's icon in the mail message.

To copy a file

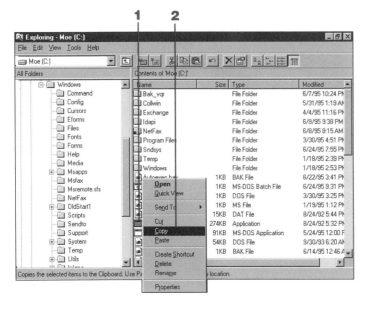

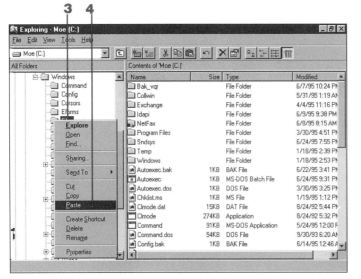

1 Right-click the file

2 Click Copy

Tip To move instead of copy, click the Cut command instead of the Copy command.

Tip To select multiple files for file operations, hold down the Ctrl key as you click each file. To select a sequence of files, click the first file and hold down the Shift key as you click the last file in the sequence.

3 Right-click the destination folder or drive

4 Click Paste

Tip You also can copy a file to a floppy disk by ckicking the file, and then choosing File, Send To, 3 1/2 Floppy.

To create a shortcut

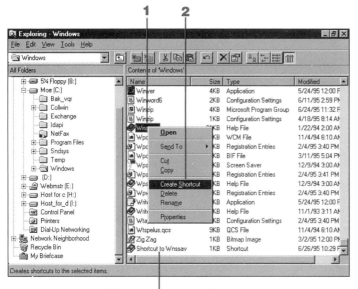

The shortcut is created

1 Right-click the file

2 Click Create Shortcut

Tip The shortcut may be copied or moved to another folder or the desktop, if desired.

To delete a file

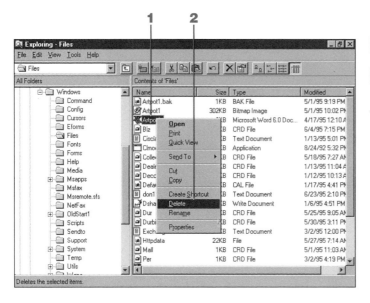

1 Right-click the file

2 Click Delete

Tip Multiple files can be selected for deletion. Use Shift+Click to select groups of adjacent files. Use Ctrl+Click for nonadjacent files.

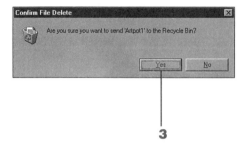

3 Click Yes to confirm
deletion

To restore a deleted file

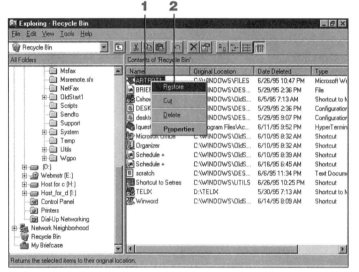

1 Right-click the file in
the Recycle Bin folder

2 Click Restore

The file is restored to its original location

Note

The Recycle Bin can also be run from the Recycle Bin icon on
the desktop. You can restore a file by highlighting it in the
Recycle Bin window and choosing File, Restore.

To rename a file or folder

1 **2**

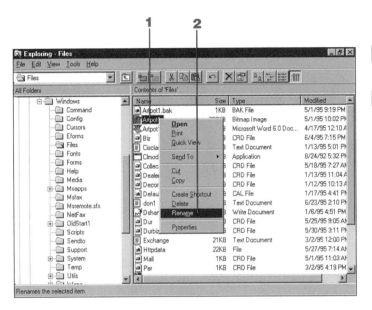

1 Right-click the file or folder

2 Click Rename

3

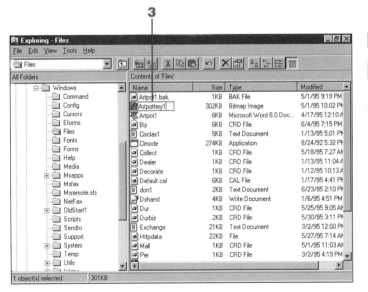

3 Type the new name

4 Press Enter

Tip The new name must be different from any name in the current folder.

To view or set file properties

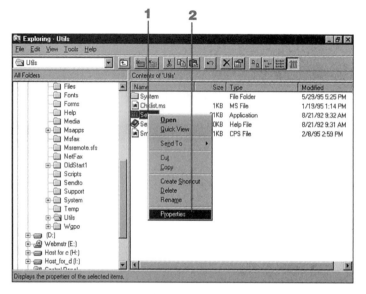

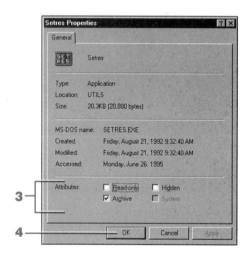

1 Right-click the file

2 Click Properties

3 Make the desired selections

4 Click OK

Note

Certain file types will display additional tabbed pages of properties in the Properties dialog box.

To add a program shortcut to the Programs menu

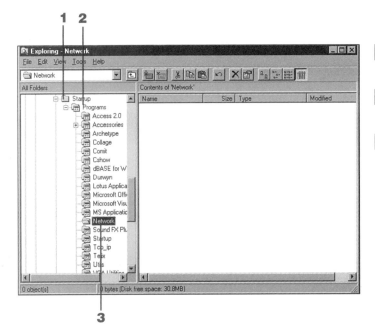

1 Double-click the Startup folder

2 Double-click the Programs folder

3 Double-click the destination folder

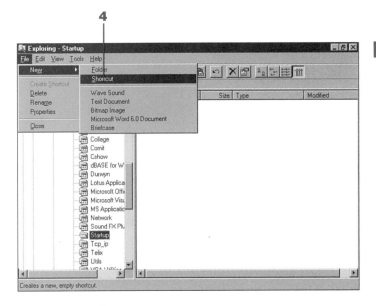

4 Choose File, New, Shortcut

121

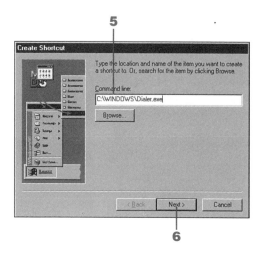

5 Type the command line for the file

6 Click Next

Tip If the command line is not known, click Browse to find the file.

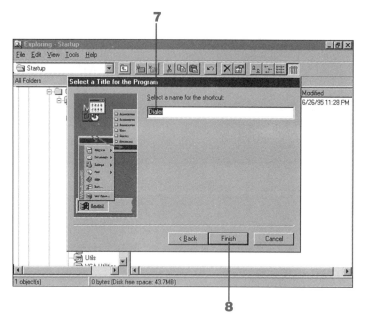

7 Type a different short-cut name, if desired

8 Click Finish

The program shortcut appears in the Programs menu in the appropriate folder

Finding Files

Use the Explorer to locate files you are unable to find. You can specify search criteria to narrow the search.

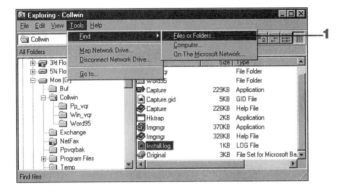

1 Choose Tools, Find, Files or Folders

To search by name and location

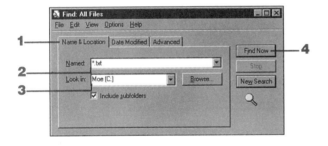

1 Click the Name & Location tab, if necessary

2 Type the name of the files you want to find

3 Select the drive or folder where you want to look

4 Click Find Now

123

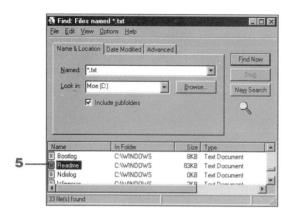

5 Double-click a file to open it

Tip You can use the wild-card characters * and ? when searching for files.

To search by date modified

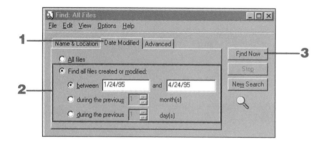

1 Click the Date Modified tab

2 Enter the search criteria

3 Click Find Now

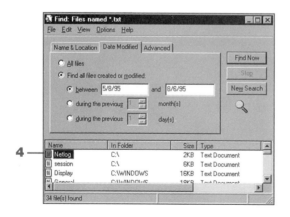

4 Double-click a file to open it

Tip If you don't find the file(s), you may need to supply more specific criteria. See the next section.

To search with advanced criteria

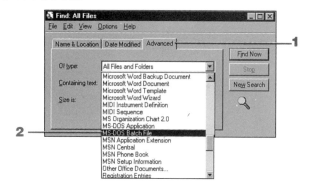

1 Click the Advanced tab

2 Select the type of file you want to find

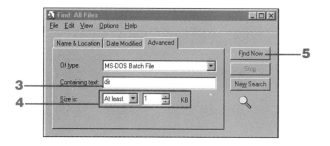

3 Type the text to search for

4 Enter the file size parameters, if desired

5 Click Find Now

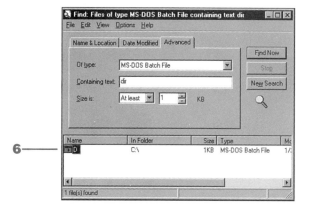

6 Double-click a file to open it

Tip Making the search criteria as specific as possible will help to reduce the search time.

Associating Files with Programs

To open a file by double-clicking it, it must be associated with an appropriate application. Most file types are associated by default, but you may need to supply some on your own.

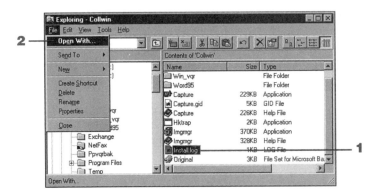

1 Select a file

2 Choose File, Open With

Tip In step 1, double-clicking the file immediately opens the dialog box shown in step 3.

Note

If the File menu contains the Open command rather than Open With, the selected file already has an association.

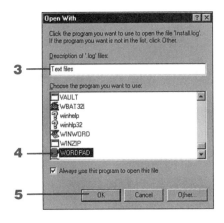

The file will open

3 Type a description

4 Select an application

5 Click OK

Changing the Explorer View

The Explorer can display lists of files in different ways. File lists can be displayed with different icons, with detail, and can be sorted.

To display with large icons

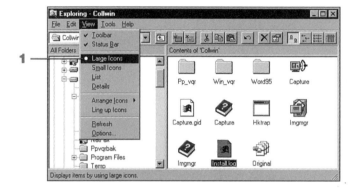

1 Choose View, Large Icons

Tip Large icons are the easiest to read.

To display with small icons

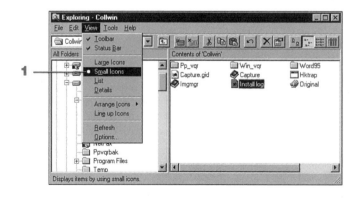

1 Choose View, Small Icons

Tip Use small icons to display the maximum number of icons in the window.

127

To display a listing

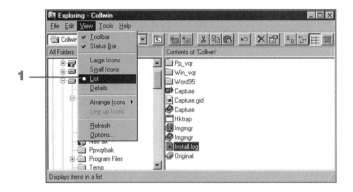

1 Choose View, List

Tip The list option displays small icons in a single column.

To display details

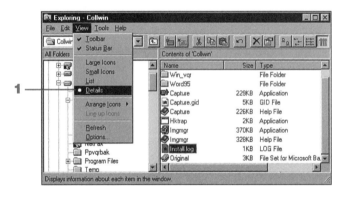

1 Choose View, Details

Tip Displaying with details will show file size, file type, and date modified.

To sort the display

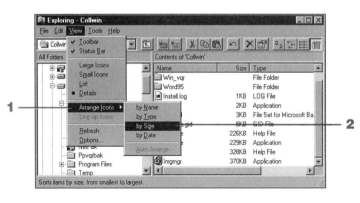

1 Choose View, Arrange Icons

2 Choose a sorting type

Tip Sorting displays files and folders in any of four logical orders.

128

Getting Help on the Desktop

If you can't remember how to perform a task, use Windows Help to get information. Windows offers many ways to get help. The primary way to access Help is through the Start menu.

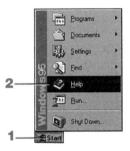

1 Click Start

2 Click Help

To use the Help Index

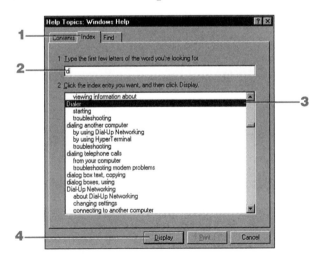

1 Click the Index tab

2 Type the topic to search for

3 Click the index entry you want to read

4 Click Display

Tip There may be a delay as Help gathers information to display.

Note

When you're typing the topic's name, the Help index jumps to different or subsequent topics as you add more letters to the topic line.

129

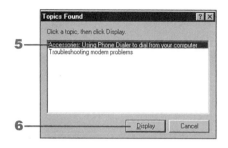

5 Select the specific topic you want

6 Click Display

Tip If there is only one topic, Windows will skip steps 5 and 6.

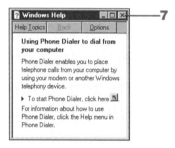

7 Click the Close button when finished

Tip Many topics, like this one, have a button that starts a related program.

To use the Table of Contents

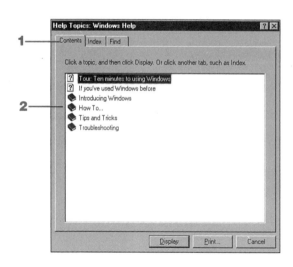

1 Click the Contents tab

2 Double-click the icon for the topic you want to open

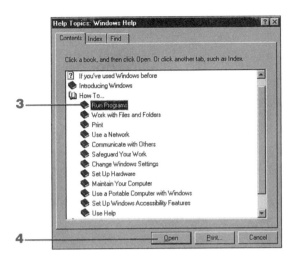

3 Click the icon for the topic you want to open

4 Click Open

Note

When a book icon is selected, you can click the Print button to print all of the topics in the book. This is a large amount of information and can take a long time to print.

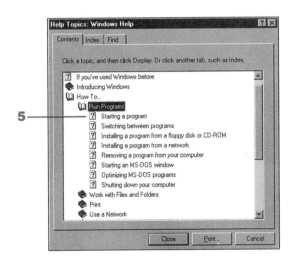

5 Click the topic you want to read; the Close button changes to a Display button

Tip Click Print to print the text of the selected topic on the default printer.

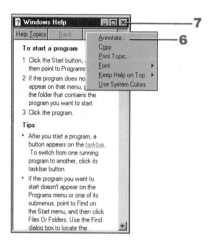

6 Click the Options button to choose options, if desired

7 Click the Close button when finished

Tip From the Options menu, you can annotate the topic, copy it to the Clipboard, or print it. Other options change the appearance of Windows Help.

Getting Help in a Dialog Box

Many dialog boxes in Windows applications have Help and ? buttons to display help that directly relates to the object being used or the action being performed.

To get help in a dialog box

1 Click Help

Note

Applications vary in the way that they offer help to the user. Different applications may place the Help button in different locations or not show it at all.

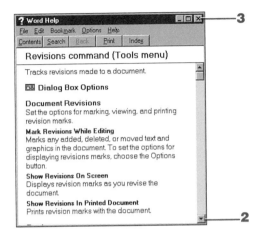

2 Scroll through the topic as necessary

3 Click the Close button when finished

Caution Help uses Windows resources. If memory is low, other applications may run slower while Help is running.

To get information in a dialog box

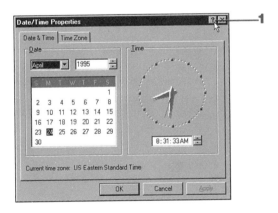

1 Click the ? help button

The pointer changes to an arrow and question mark

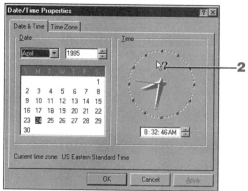

2 Click an object to display its Help information

Tip Not all objects in dialog boxes will have Help information available for them.

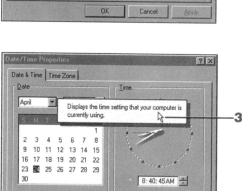

3 Click the information box to close it

Getting Help in a Window

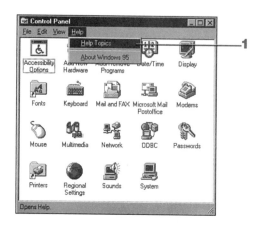

1 Choose Help, Help Topics; Windows Help is displayed

2 Click the Close button when finished

Getting Help with an Object

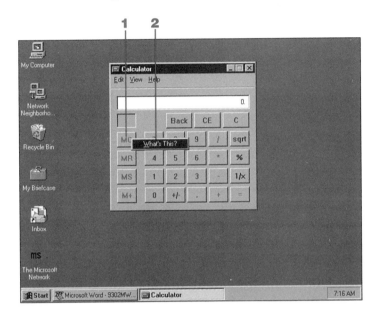

1 Right-click the object

2 Click the What's This box

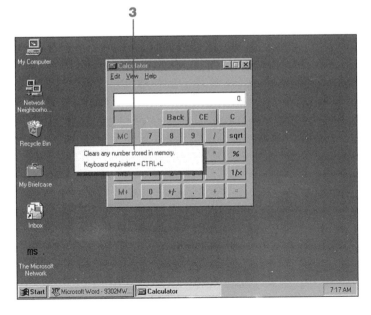

3 Click anywhere to continue

Tip The information box displays a brief explanation of the object.

Using the Inbox

Microsoft Exchange manages the creation and receipt of messages, e-mail, and faxes from different information services. The Inbox provides a central location for the management of these documents.

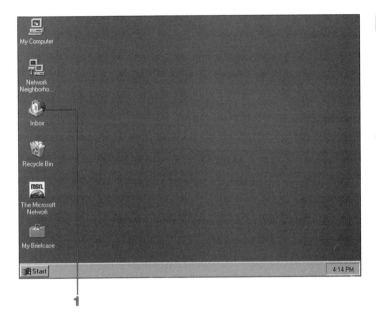

1 Double-click the Inbox icon on the desktop

Tip Another way to access the Inbox is to choose Start, Programs, Microsoft Exchange.

Note

For the Inbox to work correctly, Microsoft Exchange properties must be fully configured. The modem must be powered, configured, and online to send or receive messages from remote services.

Note

You may be asked to provide passwords or other information as Microsoft Exchange accesses folders, mailboxes, and connects to remote services. These procedures will vary according to your system configuration.

To read a message

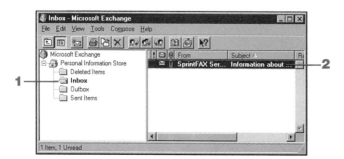

1 Click the Inbox folder, if necessary

2 Double-click a message

Note

Microsoft Exchange will route messages, faxes, and e-mail messages from online services to the Inbox folder. You can read each type of message by double-clicking it.

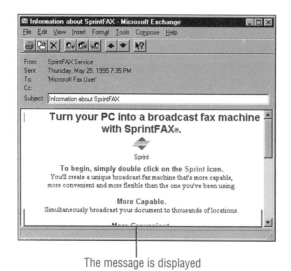

The message is displayed

To save the message

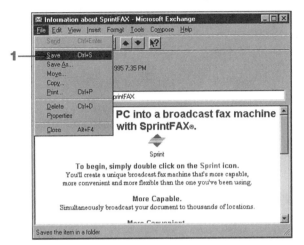

The message is saved to the default folder

1 Choose File, Save

Tip Choose File, Save As
to save the file to a
different location.

To reply to a message

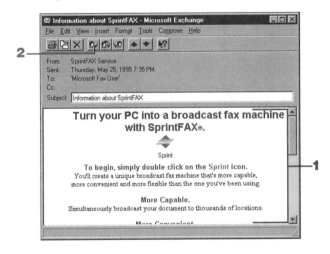

1 Display the message

2 Click the Reply to
Sender button

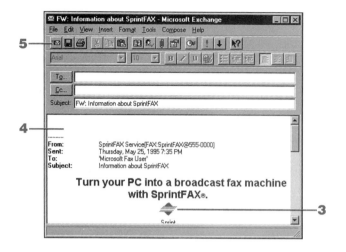

The reply is sent

3 Delete any unneeded text from the original message

4 Type your reply

5 Click the Send button

Tip Click the Cc button to choose other addresses to copy the reply to.

Note

The reply is in the same format as the original message. For example, a fax is used to reply to a fax.

To forward the message

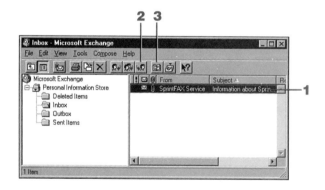

1 Select the message

2 Click the Forward button

3 Click to enter address(es) from address lists

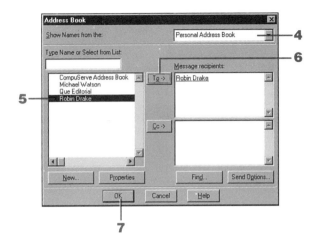

4 Select an address book

5 Select a name

6 Click To

7 Click OK

Tip Click New to add a new name and address to the list.

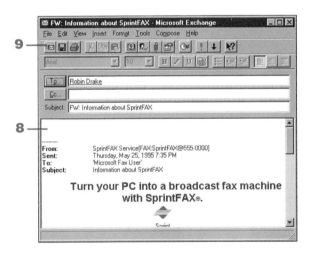

The message is sent

8 Edit the message, if desired

9 Click the Send button

To delete a message

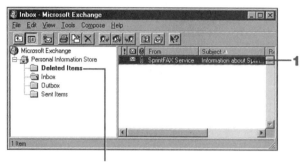

1 Select the message

2 Press the Delete key

The message is moved to the Deleted Items folder

Note

Deleted messages are automatically placed in the Deleted Items folder. To access deleted messages, double-click the Deleted Items folder. The messages may be dragged to other folders or double-clicked in order to view them.

To send a new message

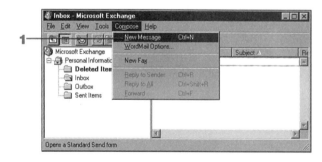

1 Choose Compose, New Message

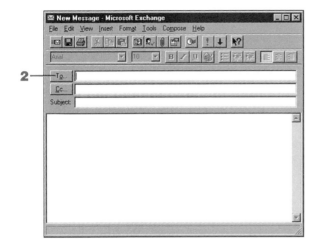

2 Click the To button

The recipient is added

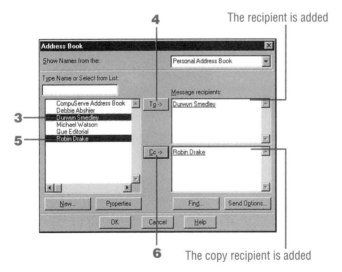

3 Select a recipient

4 Click the To button (repeat for all recipients)

5 Select recipient(s) to copy the message to, if desired

6 Click the Cc button (repeat for all people being copied on the message)

The copy recipient is added

Note

Click New to create a new address. To edit an existing address, select a name in the list box and click Properties.

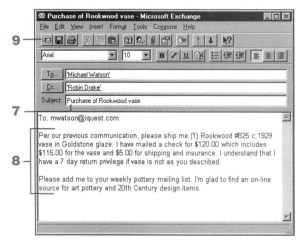

The message is sent

7 Type the subject of the message

8 Type the text of the message

9 Click the Send button

Note

Files and objects may be inserted into the message. After positioning the insertion point, choose Insert, File to insert an existing file. Choose Insert, Message to insert an existing message from a folder. Choose Insert, Object to create and insert a new OLE object.

To send a fax

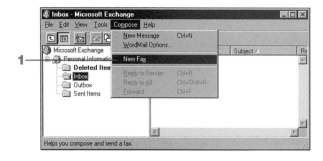

1 Choose Compose, New Fax

Note

You may be asked to provide passwords or other information as Microsoft Exchange accesses folders, mailboxes, and connects to remote services. These procedures will vary according to your system configuration.

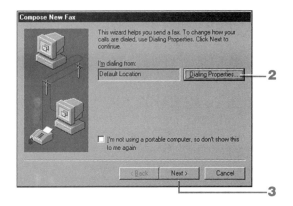

2 Click Dialing Properties to change the location, if necessary

3 Click Next

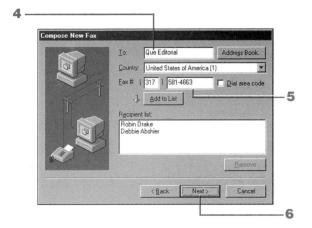

4 Type the recipient's name

5 Type the fax number

6 Click Next

Tip Click Address Book to select one or more recipients from an address book.

Note

As shown in the preceding figure, you may create a recipient list for the new fax. For each recipient, type the name and fax number and click Add to List.

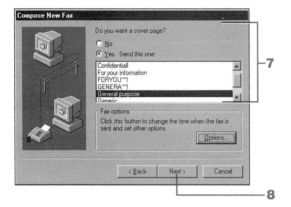

7 Select a cover page, if desired

8 Click Next

Note

Click the Options button to set fax properties. These properties are detailed later in this section.

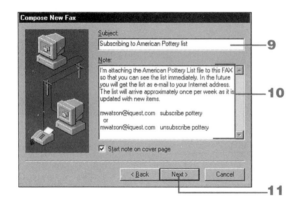

9 Type a subject

10 If desired, type a note for the cover page

11 Click Next

Note

Unless you attach a file to the fax, the note comprises the text of your fax. If you don't need to attach a file, skip to Step 16.

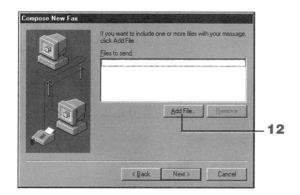

12 Click Add File

13

13 Select the drive and folder

14 Select the file

15 Click Open

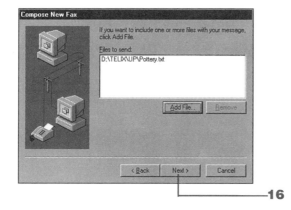

16 Click Next

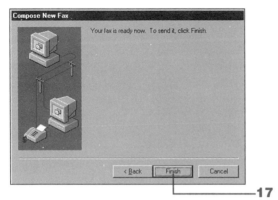

The fax is sent

17 Click Finish

To set Inbox options

1 Choose Tools, Options

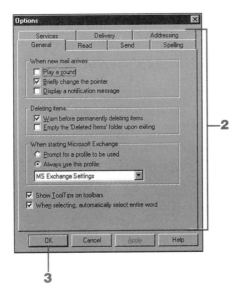

2 Set options as desired

3 Click OK

Tip Click Font on the Read tab to set the font for reply text. This visually differentiates the reply text from the original text of the message.

Note

Mail importance is a priority setting. If mail is queued in the Outbox, the messages will be sent in order of importance or priority. The Set Importance option on the Send tab controls this feature.

Note

Message services were originally configured using procedures in the "Equipment" section. Refer to that section for information about message services properties.

Using the Microsoft Network

Windows 95 provides easy access to Microsoft Network. This online service offers information forums, e-mail, and file libraries to all registered users.

To connect to Microsoft Network

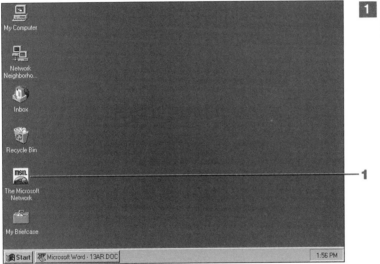

1 Double-click the Microsoft Network icon on the desktop

Note

To enable the messaging features of Microsoft Network, Microsoft Exchange properties must be fully configured.

Caution The modem must be powered, configured, and on-line to connect to Microsoft Network.

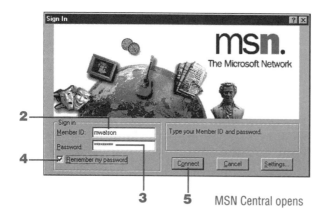

MSN Central opens

2 Type your member ID

3 Type your password

4 Click this option if you want to save your password

5 Click Connect

Note

Click Settings to change the Microsoft Network access number, dialing location, dialing properties, and modem settings. Typically, these items were configured when you installed Windows. Refer to the "Equipment" section later in this book for more information on these configuration settings and properties.

Note

Microsoft Network is an on-line service that charges a fee for access. During your first connection you will be asked for personal and credit card information in order to register and access the service.

To access MSN Today

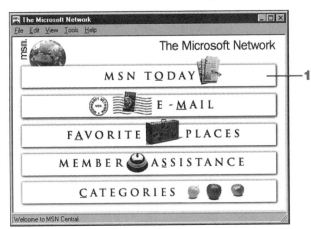

1 Click MSN Today

Tip When you log in, MSN Today is displayed by default. MSN Today shows information about new topics and the dates and times when they are available.

Click Go To to select another area to jump to

2 If desired, click a graphic image to jump to that item

3 Choose File, Exit when you want to return to MSN Central

Note

Click Calendar of Events to display a list of system events.
Click the cyan-colored text of a topic to jump to its location.

To use e-mail

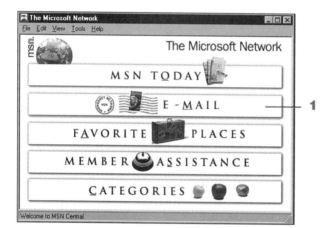

1 **Click E-Mail**

Note

Microsoft Exchange opens when you access your e-mail.
You may be asked to provide passwords or other information as Microsoft Exchange accesses folders, mailboxes, and
connects to remote services. These procedures will vary
according to your system configuration.

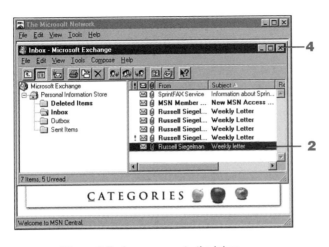

Microsoft Exchange opens to the Inbox

2 Double-click a message to read it

3 When finished, click the Close button in the message window

4 Click the Close button in the Inbox window to close the Inbox

To use items stored in Favorite Places

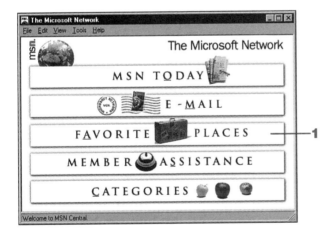

1 Click Favorite Places

Note

Favorite Places is used to hold items that you want quick access to. Any item may be copied to Favorite Places by selecting the item(s) and choosing File, Add to Favorite Places. By default, Favorite Places is empty until you add items to it.

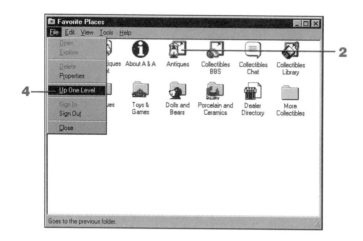

2 Double-click an item to open it

3 Close the item when finished

4 Choose File, Up One Level to return to MSN Central

To use Member Assistance services

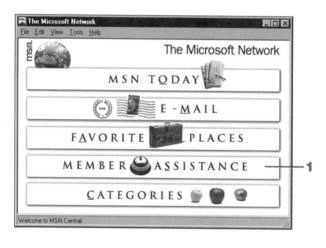

1 Click Member Assistance

Tip Member Assistance is the place to find information about using Microsoft Network.

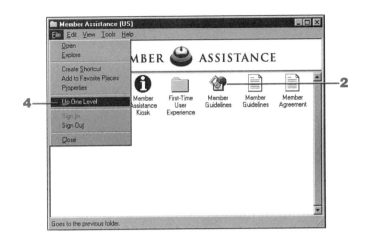

2 Double-click an item

3 Close the item when finished

4 Choose File, Up One Level to return to MSN Central

To read the bulletin boards

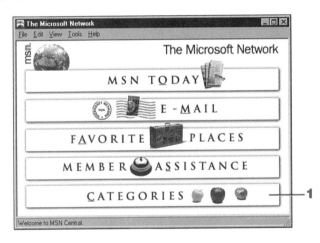

1 Click Categories

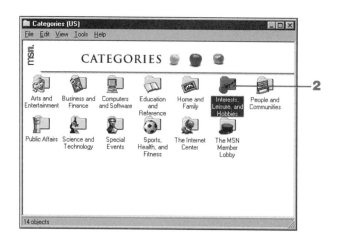

2 Double-click a folder

Tip Bulletin boards have many nested folders that organize subject matter.

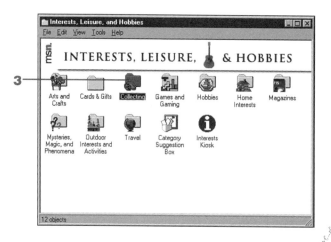

3 Double-click additional folders, if necessary

Tip The number of nested folders will vary according to the bulletin board and the subject.

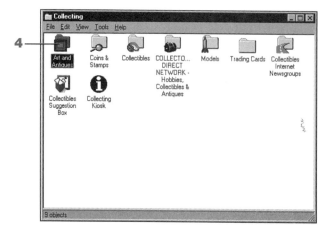

4 Continue double-clicking folders until you reach the bulletin board you want

To read a bulletin board message

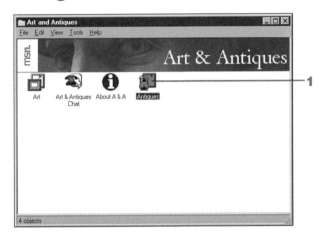

Double-click a bulletin board icon

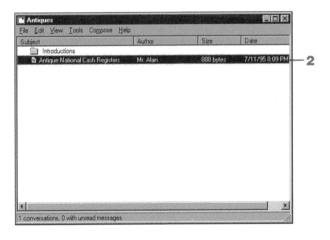

2 Double-click a message to open it in a window

Tip Some messages are contained in folders. Double-click the folder to access these messages.

The message opens in a window

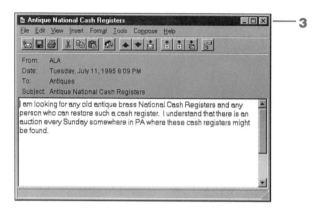

— 3

3 When finished, click the Close button in the message window

4 Click the Close button to close the bulletin board when you're done reading and posting messages

Note

To reply to a posted message, choose Compose and then choose one of the commands from the submenu. Reply to BBS will post your reply to the Bulletin Board. Reply by E-mail will reply directly to the sender. Forward by E-mail will forward to the sender or another address.

To post a bulletin board message

2 —

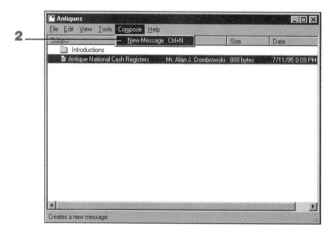

1 Open the appropriate bulletin board

2 Choose Compose, New Message

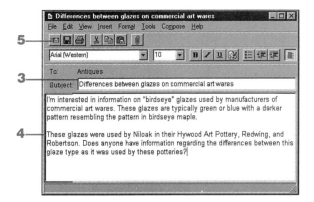

3 Type a subject

4 Type the message text

5 Click the Post button

Tip New messages are created and sent using the same basic procedures that are used in Microsoft Exchange.

Note

You may use the toolbar to change fonts and use formatting features in the text of the message. The recipient must be using Windows or a compatible program to see the message in its formatted state. Other programs will display the received message as unformatted text.

Using Windows Multimedia Accessories

Multimedia accessories are small applications that can reproduce audio CD, sound, MIDI, and video files. Typically, these accessories are run from the Start menu.

To start and close an accessory program

1 Click Start

2 Click Programs

3 Click Accessories

4 Click Multimedia

5 Click the name of the program you want

6 When you finish with the accessory program, click the Close button

Using CD Player

The CD Player accessory can be used to play audio compact discs on a system equipped with a sound card and speakers or headphones. CD Player will run as a background task and play CDs while you run other programs.

To create a play list

1 Insert an audio CD

2 Choose Start,
Programs,
Accessories,
Multimedia, CD
Player

3 Select the CD drive,
if necessary

4 Choose Disc, Edit
Play List

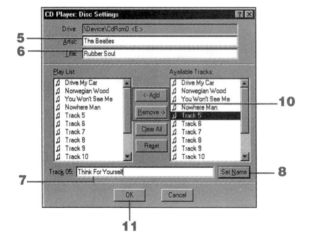

5 Type the artist's name

6 Type the CD title

7 Type the track title

8 Save the track name

9 Repeat steps 7 and 8
for each track title

10 Add and remove
tracks from play list
as desired

11 Click OK

12 Click to play

Tip Some audio CDs auto-
matically load CD
Player and play when
they are inserted.

To control CD Player

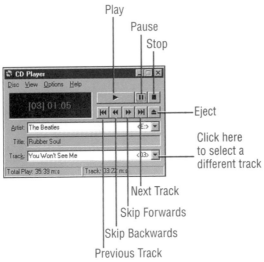

Play

Pause

Stop

Eject

Click here
to select a
different track

Next Track

Skip Forwards

Skip Backwards

Previous Track

Tip To play tracks in random order, choose Options, Random Order. To return to sequential play, choose Options, Random Order again.

Tip To play brief introductions of songs, choose Options, Intro Play. The first few seconds of each song are played.

Using Media Player

You can play sound, MIDI, CD audio, and AVI video files with Media Player.

To play a media file

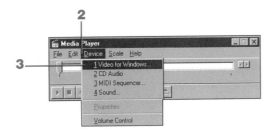

1 Choose Start, Programs, Accessories, Multimedia, Media Player

2 Choose Device

3 Choose a device to play the files

You must have an audio CD in the CD drive to use
the CD Audio device. You will get an error
message if the drive contains a data CD or
is empty.

4 Open the folder
containing the media
file to play

5 Click the file

6 Click Open

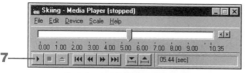

7 Click the Play button
to play

Tip The Sound, MIDI
Sequencer, and CD
Audio devices do not
open an additional
window when files
are played.

If you do not have headphones connected to the CD
drive, you must have a sound card or speaker dri-
ver installed and configured to play audio CDs or
sound files.

To control Media Player

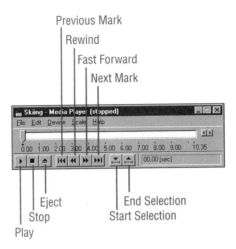

Previous Mark
Rewind
Fast Forward
Next Mark

Eject
Stop
Play
End Selection
Start Selection

Using Sound Recorder

Sound files may be recorded, modified, and played with Sound Recorder. Volume and speed may be controlled, and echo and reverse effects may be added to files.

To operate Sound Recorder

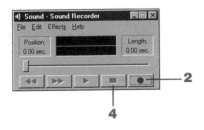

1 Choose Start, Programs, Accessories, Multimedia, Sound Recorder

2 Click the Record button to record

3 Speak into the microphone or activate the sound source

4 Click the Stop button when finished

167

To control Sound Recorder

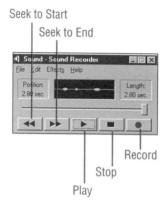

Seek to Start

Seek to End

Record

Stop

Play

To add effects

1 ──

── 2

The effect changes any subsequent playback of the sound file

1 Choose Effects

2 Choose an effect

Note _____

Effects can change volume, add echo, change speed, and play files in reverse. You can play a file with these effects, but they will make no permanent changes until you save the file. To abandon any changes to the file, exit without saving.

To save a sound file

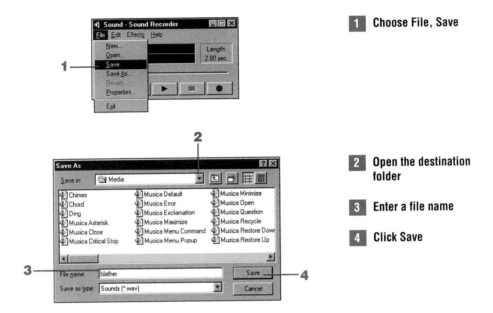

1 Choose File, Save

2 Open the destination folder

3 Enter a file name

4 Click Save

Using Volume Control

Volume Control is used to control the sound level when audio files are played through headphones or speakers. Features such as fading and muting may also be controlled.

To operate Volume Control

Note

The Volume Control accessory cannot override the maximum setting of the volume control that is physically present on your sound card. The physical volume control sets the maximum sound level that the system can attain.

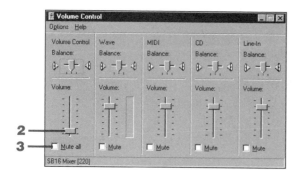

1 Right-click the Volume Control icon (on the Taskbar)

2 Drag the sliders as desired to adjust volume

3 Click the Mute option(s) to mute (silence) the sound level

Note

If you click the Volume Control icon (rather than right-clicking it), you get a single volume control level and mute option, with which you can control the overall volume setting.

Printing a File

Files are most easily printed from the application used to create them. If a file is associated with an application, it may also be printed by dragging the file to a printer icon.

To print a file by dragging and dropping

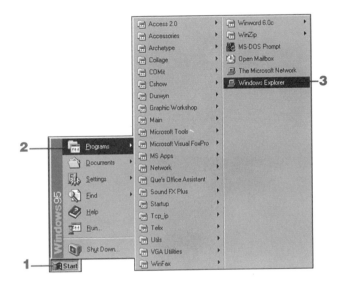

1 Click Start

2 Click Programs

3 Click Windows Explorer

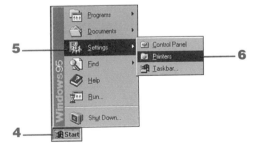

4 Click Start

5 Click Settings

6 Click Printers

Tip Windows Explorer will move to the background when you open the Printers window.

171

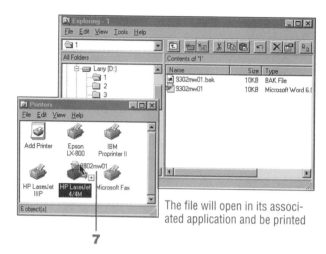

7 Drag a printable file from the Explorer to a printer icon

Tip You can send a file as a fax by dragging the file to the Microsoft Fax icon in the Printers window.

The file will open in its associated application and be printed

Controlling Your Print Jobs

When printing a file, Windows allows more control of the print job than some applications do. You can pause, resume, or cancel a current print job.

To pause a print job

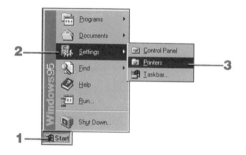

1 Click Start

2 Click Settings

3 Click Printers

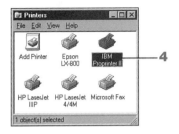

4 Double-click the printer icon

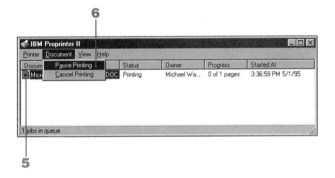

5 Click the document you want to pause

6 Choose Document, Pause Printing

Tip If you print to a network printer, the networking software controls printing. You may not be able to pause or cancel print jobs.

To resume printing a paused print job

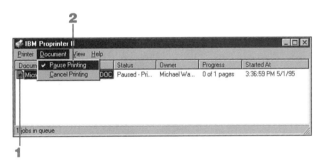

1 In the printer window, click the paused print job

2 Choose Document, Pause Printing (this option is a toggle)

To cancel a print job

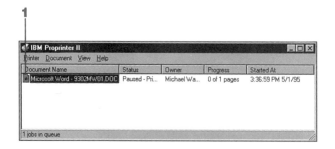

1 In the printer window, click the print job you want to cancel

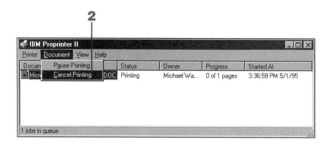

2 Choose Document, Cancel Printing

Note

Canceling a print job does not remove it from memory. The print job remains in the print queue and can still be sent to the printer. To remove a print job from memory, see "To purge print jobs" later in this section.

Caution You may not be able to cancel all print jobs.
If the printer can hold the entire document in memory, the print job will appear in the printer's window only long enough to send it to the printer.

174

To check the status of print jobs

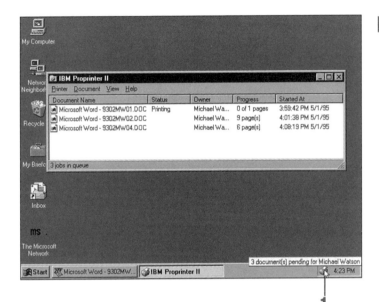

1 Point to the Print Manager icon in the Taskbar

To purge print jobs

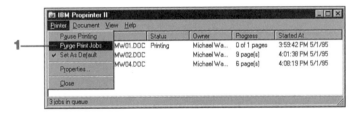

1 In the printer window, choose Printer, Purge Print Jobs

All print jobs are removed from memory

Caution You may not be able to purge all print jobs. If the printer can hold all the documents in memory, the print jobs will appear in the printer's window only long enough to send them to the printer.

Using the Windows System Accessories

The system accessories are utilities used to perform maintenance on your system. Typically, accessories are run from
the Start menu.

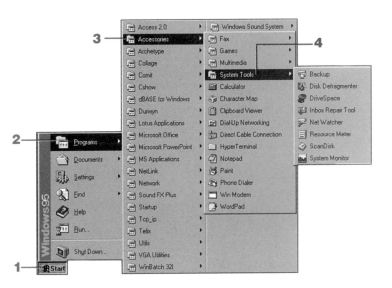

1 Click Start

2 Click Programs

3 Click Accessories

4 Click System Tools

Using Backup

Backup allows you to archive files to floppy disks, tape, or
a hard drive. The files may be restored or compared to the
originals, if needed.

To make a backup

1 Click Start, Programs,
Accessories, System
Tools, Backup

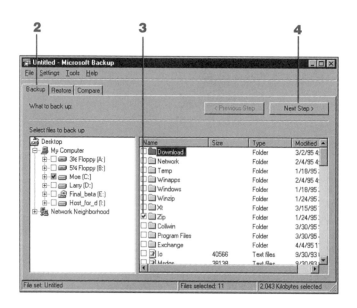

2 Click the Backup tab, if necessary

3 Select files for backup

4 Click Next Step

Tip Depending on your configuration, Backup may display additional dialog boxes.

Note

Select by clicking on appropriate check boxes. You may select files, folders, or drives for the backup. To select a group of adjacent files, click the first file and Shift+click the last file. To select a group of nonadjacent files, Ctrl+click each file.

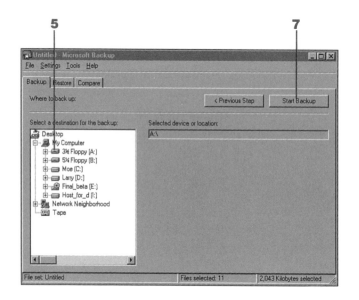

5 Select a destination

6 Insert media, if using floppy or tape

7 Click Start Backup

Tip You cannot select more than one destination.

Note

It is best to use a tape drive as the destination when backing up large groups of files, such as all files on a drive or computer.

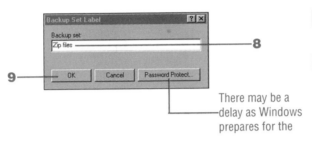

8 Type a name to assign to the backup set

9 Click OK

There may be a delay as Windows prepares for the

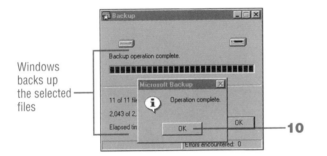

Windows backs up the selected files

Tip There may be a delay as Windows prepares for the backup operation.

10 Click OK

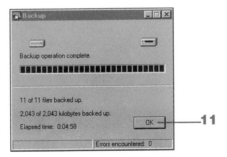

11 Click OK

To restore from a backup

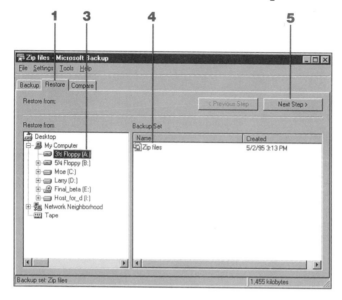

1. Click the Restore tab

2. Insert media, if using floppy or tape

3. Select source to restore from

4. Select backup set

5. Click Next Step

Note

If the backup set is password-protected, Windows will prompt for a password.

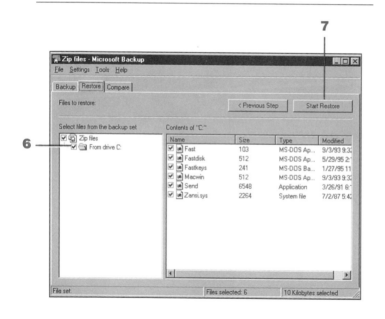

6. Select files from backup set

7. Click Start Restore

Windows restores the backup set

8. Click OK

9. Click the Close button

Defragmenting Disks with Disk Defragmenter

The Disk Defragmenter makes your hard disk more efficient by making each file contiguous and making free space contiguous.

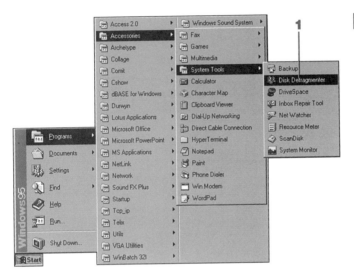

1 Click Start, Programs, Accessories, System Tools, Disk Defragmenter

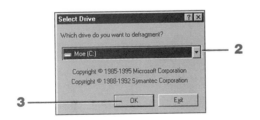

2 Select a drive to defragment

3 Click OK

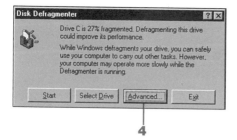

4 Click Advanced

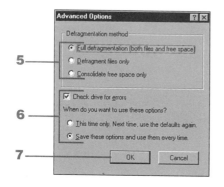

5 Select a defrag-
mentation method

6 Select options as
desired

7 Click OK

8 Click Start

Caution   If disk errors are encountered, Windows will stop
the defragmentation and prompt you to fix the
errors. Click Help in the dialog box to get
more information.

9 Click Yes when finished

Using DriveSpace

Using DriveSpace "compresses" data and allows a disk to store more files than it previously could.

1 Click Start, Programs, Accessories, System Tools, DriveSpace

Tip There may be a delay as Windows reads drive information.

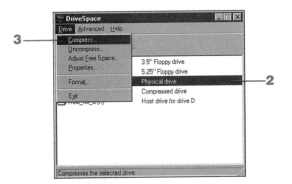

2 Select the drive to compress

3 Choose Drive, Compress

183

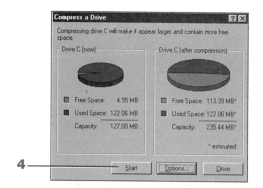

4 Click Start

Tip Click Options to view information about the access host drive, which is created during compression.

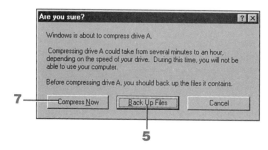

5 Click Back Up Files

6 Perform the backup operation

7 Click Compress Now

Tip You can skip the back-up in steps 5 and 6 if you have already backed up your data. Be sure you have a *good* backup before compressing your disk!

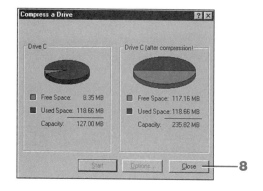

8 Click Close

9 Click the Close button in the DriveSpace window

Scanning a Disk for Errors with ScanDisk

ScanDisk examines the files, folders, and surface of your disk and repairs errors that it finds.

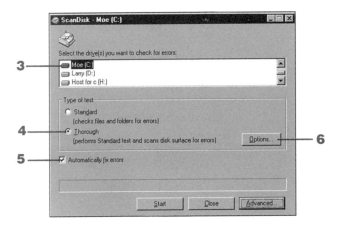

1 Click Start, Programs, Accessories, System Tools

2 Click ScanDisk

3 Select the drive to test

4 Click Thorough

5 Click Automatically Fix Errors

6 Click Options

To perform a complete scan

Note

For a quicker, less thorough scan, click Standard. This tests only files and folders, and doesn't perform the time-consuming test of the disk surface.

185

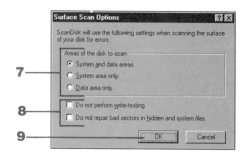

7 Select disk area to scan

8 Select other options, if desired

9 Click OK

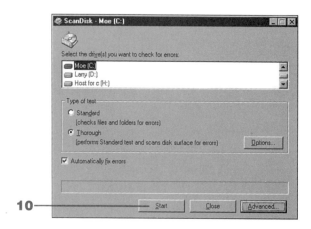

10 Click Start

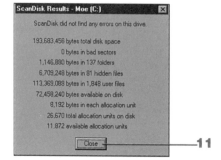

11 Click Close if a report is displayed

To customize the scan

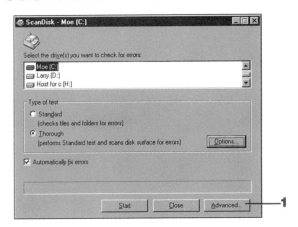

1 Click the Advanced button in the ScanDisk window

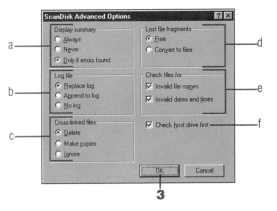

2 Select the desired options (see table)

3 Click OK

Tip The ScanDisk report can give you a useful perspective on the way your disk is utilized. If you have more folders than you thought you had, think of ways to reduce these numbers to achieve a simpler desktop.

Option	Description
a	It's a good idea to enable a summary report. The report contains information regarding the disk's structure and contents.
b	Logging options
c	Cross-link options
d	Lost file options
e	File checking options
f	Click to check host of a compressed drive first

Index

A

acceleration, hardware, 103
Accessibility icon (Control Panel)
  Display tab, 106
  General tab, 107
  Keyboard tab, 105
  Mouse tab, 107
  Sound tab, 106
accessibility options
  display, 106
  general, 107
  keyboard, 105
  mouse, 107
  sound, 106
accessories
  Calculator, 3-4
  communications
    HyperTerminal, 35-45
    Phone Dialer, 46
    mail, 47
  multimedia
    CD Player, 163, 165
    Media Player, 166-167
    Sound Recorder, 167-169
    Volume Control, 169
  Notepad, 5
    copying text, 6
    finding text, 7
    opening files, 8
    printing files, 8
    saving files, 8-9
  Paint, 10-11
    Brush, 12
    erasing, 14-15
    Eraser tool, 13
    Fill with Color tool, 12
    Line tool, 13
    starting/closing, 3
    Text tool, 14
  WordPad, 17
    bullets, inserting, 23
    centering text, 21
    coloring text, 20
    copying text, 18
    deleting text, 17
    finding text, 17
    formatting text, 19-20
    justifying text, 20-21
    opening/saving files, 24
    printing files, 24
Add New Hardware icon (Control Panel), 81
Add/Remove Program icon (Control Panel), 49-52
applications (programs)
  deleting, 49-52
  DOS
    fonts, 77
    general properties, 76
    memory settings, 78
    program properties, 77-79
    running, 74-75
    video settings, 78
  installing/uninstalling, 49-52

  opening, 32
    from files, 112, 126
    shortcuts, 121-122
    at startup, 27
associating files, 126
audio CDs, playing, 163, 165-166
audio properties, configuring, 91

B

backup files, 177-179
  passwords, 179-180
  restoring files, 180
boldface text (WordPad), 19
Brush tool (Paint), 12
Bulletin Board Service (Microsoft Network)
  composing messages, 160-161
  reading messages, 159-160
bullets (WordPad), 23

C

Calculator, 3-4
canceling print jobs, 174
capturing text (HyperTerminal), 44-45
Categories feature (Microsoft Network),157-158
CD Player, 163, 165
CD-ROM drives, configuring, 93
CDs (audio), playing, 163, 165-166
centering text (WordPad), 21
closing
  accessories, 3
  windows, 33
  Windows 95, 28
coloring
  shapes (Paint), 12
  text (WordPad), 20
commands (DOS), 73
communications accessories
  HyperTerminal, 35
    capturing text, 44-45
    connections, 36-42
    disconnecting from remote system, 45
    downloading files, 43-44
    uploading files, 42
  Phone Dialer, 46
components
  adding/removing, 51
  configuring
    CD-ROM drives
    keyboards, 83-85, 105
    modems, 88
    mouse, 88-90, 107
compressing hard disks, 183-184
configuring
  accessibility options
    display, 106
    keyboard, 105
    mouse, 107
    sound, 106

hardware
  CD-ROM drives, 93
  keyboards, 83-85
  modems, 88
  mouse, 88-90
multimedia
  advanced settings, 93
  audio properties, 91
  CD-ROM drives, 93
  MIDI properties, 92
  video properties, 92
networks, 94-95
performance options, 102
  hardware acceleration, 103
  virtual memory, 104
printers, 96-97
  fonts, 99
  graphics quality, 103
  paper orientation, 98
  sharing, 98
connections
  HyperTerminal, 36-42
  Microsoft Network, 151-152
Control Panel
  Accessibility icon
    Display tab, 106
    General tab, 107
    Keyboard tab, 105
    Mouse tab, 107
    Sound tab, 106
  Add New Hardware icon, 81
  Add/Remove Program icon, 49-52
  Date/Time icon, 60
  Display icon, 52
    Appearance tab, 55
    Background tab, 53-54
    Screen Saver tab, 54
  Fonts icon, 56
  Keyboards icon
    General tab, 84-85
    Language tab, 84
    Speed tab, 83
  Microsoft Mail Postoffice icon, 47
  Modems icon, 88
  Mouse icon
    Buttons tab, 88
    General tab, 90
    Motion tab, 89
    Pointers tab, 89
  Multimedia icon
    Advanced tab, 93
    Audio tab, 91
    CD Music tab, 93
    MIDI tab, 92
    Video tab, 92
  Network icon, 94
    Access Control tab, 95
    Identification tab, 95
  Passwords icon, 57-59
  Printers icon, 96
    Details tab, 97
    Fonts tab, 99
    General tab, 97

Graphics tab, 103
Paper tab, 98
Sharing tab, 98
Regional Settings icon, 62-64
Dates tab, 64
Time tab, 63
System icon
Performance tab, 102-104
Copy command (Quick Menu), 116
copying
files to folders/drives, 116
floppy disks, 71
Notepad text, 6
WordPad text, 18
cover pages (faxes), 146
currency settings, 63
customizing
desktop
patterns, 53
screen savers, 54
wallpaper, 54
HyperTerminal, 39
Cut command (shortcut menu), 116

D

Date/Time icon (Control Panel), 60
dates, setting, 60, 64
deleting
applications, 49-52
files, 117-118
restoring, 118
folders, 68-69
Microsoft Exchange messages, 142
WordPad text, 17
desktop, 29
display settings, 55-56
patterns, 53
screen savers, 54
wallpapers, 54
dialog boxes, help in, 132-134
disconnecting from remote system (HyperTerminal), 45
Disk Defragmenter, 181-182
Display icon (Control Panel), 56
Appearance tab, 55
Background tab, 53-54
Screen Saver tab, 54
display options
accessibility, 106
desktop, 53-56
file lists, 127-128
DOS
applications
font settings, 77
general properties, 76, 79
memory settings, 78
program properties, 77
running, 74-75
video settings, 78
commands, 73
prompt, 73
downloading files (HyperTerminal), 43-44

drawings
coloring, 12
erasing, 13
inserting text, 14
lines, 13
shapes, 12
DriveSpace, 183-184
drives
copying files to, 116
defragmenting, 181-182
scanning, 185-187
viewing contents, 110

E

e-mail messages, 154-155
deleting, 142
forwarding, 140-141
reading, 138
replying, 139-140
saving, 139
sending, 115, 142-144
effects (Sound Recorder), 168
erasing drawings, 13
events, setting sounds to, 64
exiting
accessories, 3
Windows 95, 28
expanding
drives, 110
folders, 111
Explorer
display options, 127-128
drives, expanding, 110
e-mail, sending, 115
faxes, sending, 115
files
associating with programs, 126
copying, 116
deleting, 117-118
finding, 123-125
moving, 116
opening, 112
previewing, 114
printing, 113, 171-172
properties, 120
renaming, 119
restoring deleted files, 118
floppy disks, 69
copying to, 71
formatting, 70
folders
creating, 67-68
deleting, 68-69
expanding, 111
program shortcuts, 117
associating files, 126
Programs menu, 121-122
starting, 109

F

Favorite Places (Microsoft Network), 155
faxes
sending, 115, 145, 148, 172
cover pages, 146

files
associating, 126
backing up, 177-179
passwords, 179-180
restoring files, 180
compressing, 183-184
copying, 116
deleting, 117-118
display options, 127-128
downloading, 43-44
finding, 123-125
launching programs from, 112, 126
MIDI, 163
multiple file operations, 116
naming (Notepad), 9
opening from Explorer, 112
previewing, 114
printing
drag-and-drop method, 171-172
from Explorer, 113
WordPad, 24
renaming, 119
restoring deleted files, 118
sending as e-mail/fax, 115
setting/viewing properties, 120
sound
playing, 167-169
saving, 169
uploading, 42
finding
files, 123-125
Notepad text, 7
WordPad text, 23
floppy disks, 69
copying files to, 71
formatting, 70
folders
copying files to, 116
creating, 67-68
deleting, 68-69
icons, 32
viewing contents, 111
fonts
configuring, 99
DOS program, 77
Exchange messages, 149
installing, 56-57
WordPad, 21-22
formatting
floppy disks, 70
numbers, 62
WordPad text
boldface, 19
bullets, 23
centering, 21
coloring, 20
fonts, 21-22
italics, 19
forwarding e-mail messages, 140-141

G-H

graphics
printing quality, 103
see also drawings

hard disks
  compressing, 183-184
  defragmenting, 181-182
  scanning, 185-187
hardware
  acceleration, 103
  configuring
    keyboards, 83-85
    modems, 88
    mouse, 88-90
  installing, 81
hearing-impaired, *see*
  accessibility options
Help features
  contents, 130-132
  dialog boxes, 132-134
  index, 129-130
  objects, 135
  windows, 134
HyperTerminal, 35-36
  capturing text, 44
  connections, 36-42
    saving, 40
  disconnecting from remote
    system, 45
  downloading files, 43-44
  uploading files, 42

I-J-K-L

icons
  arranging, 32
  Control Panel icons
    Accessibility, 105-107
    Add New Hardware, 81
    Add/Remove Programs,
      49-52
    Date/Time, 60
    Display, 52-55
    Fonts, 56
    Keyboards, 83-85
    Microsoft Mail Postoffice,
      47
    Modems, 88
    Mouse, 88-90
    Multimedia, 91-93
    Network, 94-95
    Passwords, 57-59
    Printers, 96-99, 103
    Regional Settings, 62-64
    System, 102-104
  Inbox, 27
  viewing files by, 127
Inbox (Microsoft Exchange), 27,
  137-140
installing
  applications, 49-52
  fonts, 56-57
  hardware, 81
  mouse, 90
italic text (WordPad), 19

justifying text (WordPad), 20

keyboards, configuring
  accessibility options, 105
  device, 84-85
  language, 84
  repeat delay, 83

Keyboards icon (Control Panel)
  General tab, 84-85
  Language tab, 84
  Speed tab, 83

left-aligning text (WordPad), 20
lines, drawing, 13

M

maximizing windows, 34
Media Player, 166-167
Member Assistance (Microsoft
  Network), 156-157
memory settings
  DOS applications, 78
  virtual memory, 104
menus, opening
  applications from, 32
messages
  bulletin board
    composing, 160-161
    reading, 159-160
  e-mail, 154-155
    deleting, 142
    forwarding, 140-141
    reading, 138
    replying, 139-140
    saving, 139
    sending, 115, 142-144
  fonts, 149
Microsoft Exchange, 115, 151,
  154-155
  Addressing tab, 149
  Delivery tab, 149
  faxes, 145, 148
    cover pages, 146
  General tab, 148
  Inbox, 137-140
  messages
    deleting, 142
    forwarding, 140-141
    reading, 138
    replying, 139-140
    saving, 139
    sending, 142-144
  Read tab, 149
  Send tab, 149
  Services tab, 149
  settings, 148-149
  Spelling tab, 149
Microsoft Mail Postoffice, 47
Microsoft Network
  Bulletin Board Service
    composing messages, 1
      60-161
    reading messages, 159-160
  Categories, 157-158
  connecting to, 151-152
  e-mail, 154-155
  Favorite Places, 155
  Member Assistance, 156-157
  MSNToday, 153-154
  settings, 152
  subscribing to, 152
MIDI
  configuring properties, 92
  files, 163

minimizing windows, 34
modems
  configuring, 88
  Hyperterminal connection,
    36-39
  Microsoft Network
    connection, 151-152
  Phone Dialer setup, 46
mouse
  accessibility options, 107
  installing, 90
  operating, 29-30
    sizing/moving windows,
      30-31
  settings
    buttons, 88
    motion, 89
    pointers, 89
Mouse icon (Control Panel)
  Buttons tab, 88
  General tab, 90
  Motion tab, 89
  Pointers tab, 89
multimedia
  accessories
    CD Player, 163, 165
    Media Player, 166-167
    Sound Recorder, 167-169
    Volume Control, 169
  configuring
    advanced settings, 93
    audio properties, 91
    CD-ROM drives, 93
    MIDI properties, 92
    video properties, 92
Multimedia icon (Control Panel)
  Advanced tab, 93
  Audio tab, 91
  CD Music tab, 93
  MIDI tab, 92
  Video tab, 92
My Computer
  running DOS applications,
    74-75
  see also Explorer

N-O

naming files
  Notepad, 9
  renaming, 119
Network icon (Control Panel), 94
  Access Control tab, 95
  Identification tab, 95
networks
  configuring, 94-95
  passwords, 58
  printers, 98
Notepad, 5
  copying text, 6
  finding text, 7
  opening files, 8
  printing files, 8
  saving files, 8-9
number formatting, 62

190

opening
  applications, 32
  files from Explorer, 112
  Notepad files, 8
  WordPad files, 24

P-Q

Paint, 10
  erasing, 14-15
  printing, 15-16
  saving, 16-17
  tools, 11
    Brush, 12
    Eraser, 13
    Fill with Color, 12
    Line, 13
    Text, 14
paper orientation, 98
passwords, 57-59
  backup files, 179-180
  remote administration, 58-59
patterns (desktop), 53
pausing print jobs, 172-173
performance options, 102
  hardware acceleration, 103
  printer graphics quality, 103
  virtual memory, 104
Phone Dialer, 46
playing audio CDs, 163, 165-166
previewing files, 114
print jobs
  canceling, 174
  pausing, 172-173
  purging, 175
  resuming, 173
  status, 175
printers, configuring, 96-97
  fonts, 99
  graphics quality, 103
  paper orientation, 98
  sharing, 98
printing, 8, 113
  drag-and-drop method, 171-172
  Notepad files, 8
  Paint files, 15-16
programs (applications)
  deleting, 49-52
  DOS
    fonts, 77
    general properties, 76
    memory settings, 78
    program properties, 77
    properties, 79
    running, 74-75
    video settings, 78
  installing/uninstalling, 49-52
  opening, 32
    from files, 112, 126
    shortcuts, 121-122
    at startup, 27
Programs menu program
  shortcuts, 121-122
purging print jobs, 175

R

reading messages (Microsoft Exchange), 138
recording sounds, 167-169
Regional Settings icon (Control Panel), 62-64
renaming files, 119
replying to messages (Microsoft Exchange), 139-140
restoring backup files, 180
resuming printing, 173
right-aligning text (WordPad), 21

S

saving
  desktop color schemes, 55
  HyperTerminal connections, 40
  Microsoft Exchange messages, 139
  Notepad files, 8-9
  Paint files, 16-17
  sound files, 169
  WordPad files, 24
ScanDisk feature, 185-187
screen elements (desktop), 29
screen savers, 54
searching parameters (Explorer), 123-125
security options (networks), 95
selecting windows, 33
sending files
  e-mail, 115, 142-144
  faxes, 115
settings
  background patterns, 53
  currency, 63
  date, 60, 64
  display, 55-56
  file properties, 120
  HyperTerminal, 36-39
  memory, 78
  Microsoft Exchange, 148-149
  mouse, 89
  multimedia, 91-93
  number formats, 62
  passwords, 57-59
  regional, 62-64
  screen savers, 54
  sounds, 64-65
  time, 60, 63
  wallpaper, 54
shapes, coloring, 12
sharing printers, 98
shortcuts, 117, 121-122
shutting down, 28
sight-impaired,
  see accessibility options
sizing windows, 31
Sound Recorder, 167
  adding effects, 168
  controlling, 168
  saving sound files, 169
sounds
  accessibility options, 106
  setting, 64-65

starting
  accessories, 3
  programs, 32
    from files, 112, 126
    shortcuts, 121-122
    at startup, 27
  Windows 95, 27
startup disks, 82
startup folder, 27
System icon, 102-104

T

time, setting, 60, 63
tools (Paint), 11
  Brush, 12
  Eraser, 13
  Fill with Color, 12
  Line, 13
  Text, 14

U-V

underlining text (WordPad), 20
uploading files (HyperTerminal), 42

video
  DOS application settings, 78
  files, 163
  properties, 92
viewing
  drive contents, 110
  file properties, 120
  folder contents, 111
virtual memory, 104
Volume Control, 169

W-Z

wallpaper, 54
windows
  applications opened from, 33
  arranging icons, 32
  closing, 33
  help, 134
  maximizing/minimizing, 34
  moving, 30
  opening, 32
  restoring, 34
  selecting, 33
  sizing, 31
Windows Explorer, see Explorer
Windows 95
  exiting, 28
  starting, 27
  see also accessories
WordPad, 17
  opening files, 24
  printing files, 24
  saving files, 24
  text, 17
    bullets, 23
    centering, 21
    coloring, 20
    copying, 18
    deleting, 17
    finding, 17
    formatting, 19-20
    justifying, 20-21

Look and Learn...
with Visual Quick References

Complete and Return this Card
for a *FREE* Computer Book Catalog

Thank you for purchasing this book! You have purchased a
superior computer book written expressly for your needs. To
continue to provide the kind of up-to-date, pertinent coverage
you've come to expect from us, we need to hear from you.
Please take a minute to complete and return this self-addressed,
postage-paid form. In return, we'll send you a free catalog of all
our computer books on topics ranging from word processing to
programming and the internet.

Mr. ☐　　Mrs. ☐　　Ms. ☐　　Dr. ☐

Name (first) ☐☐☐☐☐☐☐☐☐☐☐☐ (M.I.) ☐ (last) ☐☐☐☐☐☐☐☐☐☐☐☐☐

Address ☐☐☐☐☐☐☐☐☐☐☐☐☐☐☐☐☐☐☐☐☐☐☐☐☐☐☐☐☐

☐☐☐☐☐☐☐☐☐☐☐☐☐☐☐☐☐☐☐☐☐☐☐☐☐☐☐☐☐

City ☐☐☐☐☐☐☐☐☐☐☐☐☐☐☐☐☐ State ☐☐ Zip ☐☐☐☐☐ ☐☐☐☐

Phone ☐☐☐　☐☐☐　☐☐☐☐ Fax ☐☐☐　☐☐☐　☐☐☐☐

Company Name ☐☐☐☐☐☐☐☐☐☐☐☐☐☐☐☐☐☐☐☐☐☐☐

E-mail address ☐☐☐☐☐☐☐☐☐☐☐☐☐☐☐☐☐☐☐☐☐☐☐☐☐☐☐☐☐

1. Please check at least (3) influencing factors for purchasing this book.

Front or back cover information on book .... ☐
Special approach to the content .... ☐
Completeness of content .... ☐
Author's reputation .... ☐
Publisher's reputation .... ☐
Book cover design or layout .... ☐
Index or table of contents of book .... ☐
Price of book .... ☐
Special effects, graphics, illustrations .... ☐
Other (Please specify): _____ ☐

2. How did you first learn about this book?

Internet Site .... ☐
Saw in Macmillan Computer
　　Publishing catalog .... ☐
Recommended by store personnel .... ☐
Saw the book on bookshelf at store .... ☐
Recommended by a friend .... ☐
Received advertisement in the mail .... ☐
Saw an advertisement in: _____ ☐
Read book review in: _____ ☐
Other (Please specify): _____ ☐

3. How many computer books have you purchased in the last six months?

This book only .... ☐　　3 to 5 books .... ☐
2 books .... ☐　　More than 5 .... ☐

4. Where did you purchase this book?

Bookstore .... ☐
Computer Store .... ☐
Consumer Electronics Store .... ☐
Department Store .... ☐
Office Club .... ☐
Warehouse Club .... ☐
Mail Order .... ☐
Direct from Publisher .... ☐
Internet site .... ☐
Other (Please specify): .... ☐

5. How long have you been using a computer?

Less than 6 months .. ☐　　6 months to a year ..... ☐
1 to 3 years .... ☐　　More than 3 years ...... ☐

6. What is your level of experience with personal computers and with the subject of this book?

	With PC's	With subject of book
New	☐	☐
Casual	☐	☐
Accomplished	☐	☐
Expert	☐	☐

Source Code — ISBN: 1-56529-930-2

7. Which of the following best describes your job title?

Administrative Assistant .... ☐
Coordinator .... ☐
Manager/Supervisor .... ☐
Director .... ☐
Vice President .... ☐
President/CEO/COO .... ☐
Lawyer/Doctor/Medical Professional .... ☐
Teacher/Educator/Trainer .... ☐
Engineer/Technician .... ☐
Consultant .... ☐
Not employed/Student/Retired .... ☐
Other (Please specify): .... ☐

8. Which of the following best describes the area of the company your job title falls under?

Accounting .... ☐
Engineering .... ☐
Manufacturing .... ☐
Marketing .... ☐
Operations .... ☐
Sales .... ☐
Other (Please specify): .... ☐

9. What is your age?

Under 20 .... ☐
21-29 .... ☐
30-39 .... ☐
40-49 .... ☐
50-59 .... ☐
60-over .... ☐

10. Are you:

Male .... ☐
Female .... ☐

11. Which computer publications do you read regularly? (Please list)

_____
_____
_____
_____
_____
_____
_____
_____
_____
_____

Comments: _____
_____
_____

Fold here and scotch-tape to m.

⑊⁙⁙⁙⁙⁙⁙⁙⁙⁙⁙⁙